F. W. J. SCHELLING

Translated, with an introduction ... a Steinkamp

Clara

or, On Nature's Connection to the Spirit World

STATE UNIVERSITY OF NEW YORK PRESS

Published by

State University of New York Press, Albany

© 2002 State University of New York

All rights reserved

Printed in the United States of America

No part of this book may be used or reproduced in any manner whatsoever without written permission. No part of this book may be stored in a retrieval system or transmitted in any form or by any means including electronic, electrostatic, magnetic tape, mechanical, photocopying, recording, or otherwise whitout the prior permission in writing of the publisher.

For information, address
State University of New York Press,
90 State Street, Suite 700, Albany, NY 12207

Production, Laurie Searl
Marketing, Michael Compochiaro

Library of Congress Cataloging-in-Publication Data

Schelling, Friedrich Wilhelm Joseph von, 1775–1854.
    [Clara, English]
    Clara, or, On nature's connection to the spirit world / F.W.J. Schelling ; translated, with an introduction, by Fiona Steinkamp.
        p. cm. — (SUNY series in contemporary continental philosophy)
    Includes bibliographical references and index.
    ISBN 0-7914-5407-X (alk. paper) — ISBN 0-7914-5408-8 (pbk. : alk. paper)
    1. Spiritualism (Philosophy) 2. Philosophy of nature. I. Title: Clara. II. Title: On nature's connection to the spirit world. III. Title. IV. Series.

B2894.C42 E5 2002
129—dc21   2002066903

10 9 8 7 6 5 4 3 2 1

Contents

GENERAL INTRODUCTION by Fiona Steinkamp	vii
Clara—Introducing the Text	vii
Situating *Clara*—*The Ages of the World* and *Bruno*	x
Dating of *Clara*	xiii
Schelling—Biographical Details	xvii
Schelling's Early Years	xvii
Caroline—Background	xix
Schelling and Auguste	xx
Schelling and Caroline	xxiii
Schelling's Letters and Their Similarity to Clara	xxviii
Schelling and Pauline	xxxi
Who is Clara?	xxxiii
Closing Remarks	xxxv
Biographical Sources Used	xxxvi
Notes about the Translation	xxxvii
Edition Translated	xxxvii
Translation Difficulties	xxxviii
Footnotes and Endnotes	xxxix
Numbering of Sections	xxxix
Acknowledgments	xxxix
CHRONOLOGY	xli

CLARA
or, On Nature's Connection to the Spirit World

INTRODUCTION		3
I	[11]	9
II	[27]	21

III	[40]	31
IV	[86]	63
V	[92]	67
Spring	[175]	79
Sketch	[275]	83

APPENDIX 85
    German Single Editions of *Clara* 85
    Translations of *Clara* 85
    Selected Works with Substantial Discussions of *Clara* 85
    English Translations of Schelling 86

NOTES 89

GLOSSARY 97
    German-English 97
    English-German 101

REFERENCES 107

INDEX 111

GENERAL INTRODUCTION

FIONA STEINKAMP

Clara is unique in the philosophical literature. It is a discussion told as a story, its very structure reflects its content, and it has a woman as one of its central characters. Unfortunately, the work remains as only a fragment, but it is imbued with many Romantic themes and can be read on a variety of levels. This lends the discussion a certain beauty. Clara is possibly Schelling's only work that aims to make his thought more accessible and that actually succeeds in doing so, even if, ironically, Schelling never told anyone about the text. I will attempt throughout my introduction to keep to the spirit of Clara; I will leave more technical treatments for scholarly journals. In order to help readers orient themselves more easily when first reading the text, I will begin by outlining the general arguments and structure of Clara. Schelling's introduction is not included in this overview as it is so different in character from the rest of the discussions.

CLARA—INTRODUCING THE TEXT

Clara has three main characters—the priest, the doctor, and Clara. Each takes its turn at being the persuasive or leading element and each can be understood metaphorically. The priest represents arguments in favor of the mind or spirit, the doctor speaks in favor of nature and the corporeal, and Clara is personality or the soul. Appropriately, she is also the only main character with a name.

The first section begins in the autumn on All Souls' Day with the priest and the doctor coming into town to pick up Clara. Its purpose is to introduce the topic of the discussions that follow. This is also reflected by the scene—the festival in celebration of the dead; the autumnal, natural transition into winter. As indicated in Schelling's introduction, the work starts with the assumption that there is a spirit world. Schelling is not speaking to those who are not prepared to start out from this presupposition. Another assumption that runs throughout is that man is not a purely physical being—man also has a nonphysical aspect to his nature. From these two assumptions Schelling argues that a link from the physical to the spiritual can be found—the arguments in the first section are based on these two suppositions.

The priest argues that the spiritual plays too small a role in this life. He maintains that this life is too one-sided and that the spirit life needs to be made a part of it, a reminder that there is a spirit life and that the deceased are part of our larger family. The clergyman, a minor character who appears only in this section and who represents Kant (Grau 1997), argues that death should be seen as a complete separation from this life and that the deceased are dead in regard to this world. The clergyman maintains that the two worlds are completely separate and this life cannot act on the other. Moreover, he claims that we cannot properly conceive of the other (spirit) world because the spiritual aspect of man is tainted by the physical. Man can only follow his conscience, which comes from the Divine and is a proof of immortality. This is his duty in life. Clara argues that there is a link, communication, between this world and the next one. The doctor offers the view that man needs to start out from this world if he is to gain knowledge of the next one. If he proceeds in any other fashion, he will only be speculating. It is the doctor who remarks on the likenesses between the generations in the pictures at the cloister and who works from this natural similarity to the idea of the transmigration of souls.

Thus, the characters in this section provide four arguments about a spirit world and its relation to this life: the spirit world enters this life; the two worlds are kept completely separate; there is interaction between this life and the next; man can learn about the next life from looking carefully at this one. Only the clergyman argues against trying to find any connection between the two and, predictably, given that *Clara* is about nature's connection to the spirit world, the three main characters disagree with the clergyman. This first section, therefore, sets the scene for the rest of the discussions. Notably, in this introductory piece these characters have been separated and are getting together to return home. Likewise, later in *Clara* it is postulated that the three elements (body, spirit, and soul) that were originally one have become separated; their ultimate aim is to reunite.

The second section is a conversation between the doctor and Clara, with the doctor's thoughts dominating this section. This makes *Clara* consistent with the doctor's injunction in the first section that we should look first at this life before discussing the next one. The conversation begins with Clara complaining about the destructive power of nature. That is, she has lost her connection to nature. The doctor argues—in a Platonic style dialogue—that nature is essentially creative and *as* creative, it can't be destructive. Thus, there must be something foreign to nature that restricts it and that causes it to destroy; this foreign body can't be God, so it must be man. Clara asks for another style of argument, one that shows a development rather than one that uses deductive logic. The quest for a new form of argument is another theme that runs throughout *Clara*. The doctor asks to be permitted two assumptions—(1) that the natural and the spiritual worlds are to be contrasted and (2) that man is the turning point between the two worlds. Given these assumptions, nature has to find its connection to the spiritual through man. However, currently man is not directly connected to the spiritual but progresses to the spiritual only through death. He is in the external world and has turned toward nature. Thus, if the two worlds are not currently united within man, it must be because man has turned his back on the spiritual and has thus hindered nature from progressing. A discussion of chance, necessity, and freedom follows. The section ends with the thought that the more man understands the limitations of his current life, the more he will appreciate the signs of the next one within it.

The third section takes place at Christmas (also to be understood metaphorically) and this time the priest offers his views. Clara sometimes feels as if the spiritual world is already embracing her, but she cannot hold onto this state for very long. She always ends up returning to this life. That is, she cannot retain her connection to the spiritual. The priest maintains that we cannot remain in a spiritual state because our present world is imperfect. It is not possible to have a proof of the hereafter because proofs are always indirect. He argues that if the whole person survives death and if the whole person comprises body, spirit, and soul, then the transition into the spirit world is merely a change in balance between these three elements.

Appropriately, at this point the doctor comes in and all three elements are again present. Not surprisingly, the doctor contends that this life is better than the next one because it has a bodily element that the spiritual life lacks. The priest explains that it is not just that body, spirit, and soul have a different balance in the next life, but also that the new balance is better; it is a progression. Then, as if united and in equal balance, all characters discuss magnetic sleep and clairvoyance. Clara speaks about dying and going over into the spirit world—the transitional viewpoint; the doctor speaks about magnetic sleep and being transferred through that into a different realm—the physical viewpoint; and the priest, playing a lesser role, speaks about clairvoyant abilities as an indication that even this life has its spiritual side. Like Clara's feeling that the spiritual world is embracing her already, this balance and unity between the characters does not last long, and the three characters then discuss ghosts—the spirit life. Clara is horrified by the idea of ghosts, but the priest speculates that there are many intermediate realms between this life and the other world and that those who grasp on to the external world in this life will be in agony when the bodily life is taken away from them.

The fourth section champions the need for philosophy to be presented in a more accessible form, one where characters are used to bring the ideas to life.

The following section takes place between winter and spring as the three characters climb a hill. The priest thinks that the spiritual and the natural are not really opposed, and once on top of the hill he wonders what the spirit world might be like. He believes that originally spirit and nature were one. Similarly, only when the old Protestant woman is on top of the hill does she confess that she had made a vow to the Catholic St. Walderich to save her son from death. Thus, all conversations on top of the hill represent belief or, more precisely, different beliefs coming together. On coming back down the hill, the three main characters discuss the effect that belief has on the world. The approach now is not one from nature to the spirit world, but one from the spiritual/mental down to life. The former approach from nature to spirit reflects Schelling's early, "negative" philosophy, and the latter one from the spiritual to the natural is Schelling's later, "positive" philosophy. Schelling always wanted to unite the two.

In the section known as the spring fragment, set in a time of transition and growth, Clara takes the leading role. This is fitting as Clara is the only character so far who has not had her turn at taking the leading position. By spring Clara appears to have regained her connection to nature and describes herself as "nature's child." Her main concern in this section is that the soul, too, should have a chance to take the leading role, to be fulfilled. She understands that in this life nature has the leading role, that in the next life the spirit is freed, but she wonders about the soul. More than this we do not hear, for the rest of the discussion is missing. The future remains for us a mystery, as it was for Schelling.

Clara follows the seasons, and presumably after the spring fragment, summer was to follow. This final section would also have covered Clara's death, for the fact that she later dies is briefly indicated early in the work. More than this, however, we do not know.

SITUATING CLARA—THE AGES OF THE WORLD AND BRUNO

The majority of commentators believe that *Clara* is in some way connected to *The Ages of the World*; any disagreement usually revolves around *how* they are connected. *The Ages of the World* was Schelling's favorite project. He never took it to print, despite many good intentions, and kept on working on it lovingly for many years. It is now generally regarded as one of Schelling's most famous and important writings.[1] Some commentators, such as Horn (1997), believe that *Clara* was a precursor to *The Ages of the World*, others—including Schelling's son—maintain that *Clara* was the beginning of the missing third book of *The Ages of the World*. Obviously, this is not the place for a thorough consideration of this very complicated issue, but it is worth outlining some of the theories that have been offered and I will add a couple of my own.

In the original manuscripts, the spring fragment to *Clara* was located and numbered by Schelling's son to precede Schelling's introduction to the second book ("The Present") of the 1811–1812 edition of *The Ages of the World*. Horn (1997) argues that *Clara*—or at least the version of *Clara* without the spring fragment—is an intuitive outline for the whole of *The Ages of the World*. He claims that the basic concept of the discussion is the same as that which underlies *The Ages of the World*. Horn describes this basic concept as the idea of an original unity of two worlds broken by human sin. However, this description better fits the theme of Schelling's earlier *Of Human Freedom* than that of *Clara*, for *Clara*'s subject matter focuses more on how to connect to the future world (to which we go after death) from the one in which we are currently living.[2] That is, *Clara* presupposes the world in which we already live, whereas *The Ages of the World*—or at least its sole remaining first book ("The Past")—deals more with the idea of development, of the birth of God and of the world. Thus, from this perspective, *Clara* appears to be at a later stage of argument than the first book of *The Ages of the World*.

Nevertheless, in support of Horn's argument, I note that Schelling does use the idea of the original unity of the two worlds in *Clara*, and *Clara* does share several themes with *The Ages of the World*. For instance, one obvious connection is the use of the doctrine of the three potencies, which in *Clara* is represented by the interactions between the three main characters of the book. Moreover, Horn reminds us that Schelling tackled *The Ages of the World* trilogy (past, present, and future) as a whole. Thus, Horn argues, we would be mistaken to think of *Clara* as belonging to *The Ages of the World* or to date *Clara* after it just because the spring fragment was positioned at a later point. The sequence of composition does not have to follow the final intended sequence. What is placed later could still have been written first.

Schelling's son, however, believed that the *Clara* manuscript was intended as a sketch or a beginning of the third book ("The Future") of *The Ages of the World*. This view was also initially supported by Schröter. In terms of *Clara*'s content there is reason to have some sympathy with this viewpoint, although it is an opinion that lacks current popularity. If it is agreed that the main object of *Clara* is to find the connection between this world and the next, then *Clara* is at the very least a description of the transition from the present to the future. Moreover, in some places in *Clara* there is pure speculation about the future world. Of course, one could argue with Horn that *Clara* is a sketch of the whole and thus it also contains passages illustrating some of the proposed content for the third book. However, there is relatively little discussion of the past in *Clara*, and it is normally mentioned only in the sense of something to be overcome. For example, the priest and the doctor continually try to ease Clara away from thinking about the past, about Albert. And although the doctrine of the three potencies—of the rotation and interplay of two opposites and a uniting element—is present in *Clara* as it is in the first book of *The Ages of the World*, this does not necessarily indicate that what is sketched in *Clara* is an initial exposition of the latter work. For Schelling the doctrine of the potencies was basic; it is something that is repeated at all levels. Thus it should be reflected in any stage.

It is also possible to argue that *Clara* should be understood as a sketch for the second book of the trilogy. Horn himself offers this view as a possibility and K. F. A. Schelling's placement of the spring fragment may further support this interpretation. *Clara*'s philosophy (work first from this world to find the connection to the next) likewise strengthens the claim that *Clara* represents "the present"— the second book of *The Ages of the World*. Similarly, the sketch originally found on the back of the spring fragment provides a long discussion of clairvoyance. It is debatable whether this discussion has already been completed in *Clara* or whether Schelling intended to write a future section, either in *Clara* or in *The Ages of the World*, treating the question more thoroughly. If one believes that *Clara* contains Schelling's full discussion of clairvoyance, then it is better to understand *Clara* as the intended third book of *The Ages of the World*. Otherwise *Clara* is better understood as the second book, for then *Clara* emphasizes the link from the present to the future; and the future—Clara's death, for example—is never fully addressed. In *Clara* the future is merely intimated, and perhaps this is all that Schelling ever felt he could do.

Nevertheless, in addition to these complex issues, there is another view of how to situate *Clara* among Schelling's works: some commentators (Borlinghaus 1994) maintain that *Clara* was originally written as one of a series of dialogues that Schelling wanted to publish. I have been unable to find any evidence to support this view. Schelling wrote two discussions in his lifetime, both of which were published in 1802. One is the relatively little-known polemical dialogue against Reinhold in the *Kritisches Journal*, entitled "Über das absolute Identitätssystem und sein Verhältnis zu dem neuesten Dualismus. Gespräch zwischen dem Verfasser und einem Freund" ("On the system of absolute identity and its relationship to the most recent dualism. A conversation between the author and a friend"). The other is his book *Bruno*.[3] *Bruno* was supposed to be followed by two other discussions and the second one of these, which never followed, was to be entitled "Der Traum des Kirsos" ("Kirsos's dream"). However, other than the fact that *Clara*, too, is a discussion or dialogue, there is little to support the view that it belongs to *Bruno*. Two years later, in the preface to *Philosophie und Religion*, Schelling mentions that he had wanted to present the content in a discussion but that time constraints had stopped him (White 1983). *Philosophie und Religion*, he said, retained the content of the planned discussion, but not the symbolic form. The only known discussion in symbolic form by Schelling is *Clara*, so perhaps the germs of *Clara* were growing at this time. In the preface to *Philosophie und Religion* Schelling stresses that conversation is a higher form, that it cannot serve just as a means, and that it has a worth in itself. This description fits *Clara* as well. By September 1805, the theme of a discussion that Schelling had in mind was the Fall; he believed this topic to be inappropriate for a purely scientific lecture. The topic of the Fall seems more suitable for *Of Human Freedom*, which did not appear until 1809. In the preface to this work, Schelling says that he is presenting the content that he had put forth unsuccessfully in *Philosophie und Religion*. Thus, if *Philosophie und Religion* was based on a discussion, and Schelling later reworked its content, the discussion may have been reworked too. In February 1806 he announced that he would introduce a new, shorter discussion at the book fair along with *Bruno*. However, no new, shorter discussion was ever forthcoming.

Another possibility, of course, is that *Clara* is a stand-alone work and is not connected to any one particular essay. Indeed, *Schellingiana Raroria* contains Schelling's own listing of his works.[4] "Der Traum des Kirsos" is never mentioned, but in the folio Schelling explicitly mentions the beginnings of a discussion on survival and the future life. And, although he requested that *Clara* be destroyed, he also expressed the hope that his son would enjoy reading it and find something worthwhile in it. That is, *Clara* was not a work that was written in 1810 and then forgotten, or remembered only with some embarrassment; it was a work for which he obviously had some fondness right up to his death. He did hope that some of it might be of use. Moreover, the request that the work be destroyed must be seen in context. Schelling also requested that *The Ages of the World*, the *Erlangen Seminars*, and his lectures on *System of Philosophy* be destroyed. There is no mention of any connection of *Clara* either to *Bruno* or to *The Ages of the World*. Indeed, *Clara*'s form is very different from the poetic thrust of the first book of *The Ages of the World*; in this regard *Clara* seems unlikely as a continuation of that book. Moreover, *Clara* makes little mention of the past and thus does not appear to be a sketch for the entire *Ages of the World* trilogy, either. This suggests that *Clara* is a unique work not only in its philosophical form, but also in Schelling's philosophy as a whole. That is, it deserves its own special place in the philosophical literature.

DATING OF CLARA

Inextricably connected to discussions as to where to place *Clara* contextually within Schelling's works is the issue of dating the text. Thus, in believing *Clara* to be a sketch for the third book of *The Ages of the World*, Schelling's son argued that *Clara* was written in 1817. This view was challenged at the time (Beckers 1865, 23) and *Clara* is now popularly believed to have been composed in 1810, shortly after the unexpected death of Caroline, Schelling's wife, in 1809 (Beckers 1865, Gulyga 1989, Horn 1997, Kahn-Wallenstein 1959, Tilliette 1970, Vetö 1973). As many commentators have noted, there are striking similarities between some of the letters that Schelling wrote to friends shortly after his wife's death and certain passages in *Clara*. Even Schelling's son agreed that some sections of *Clara* were undoubtedly written at this time (Beckers 1865). The "Stuttgart Seminars" is also often cited to support the view that *Clara* was written in 1810.[5] These lectures, or rather small gatherings, took place in 1810 and were designed for a popular audience. Toward the end of the "Stuttgart Seminars," Schelling dealt with the theme of life after death, and *Clara* and the "Stuttgart Seminars" are often regarded as similar both in their content and in their design as more popular works.

Nevertheless, at least the idea of *Clara* may have been in Schelling's mind before Caroline's death. What reasons could there be for thinking that some of *Clara* might have been composed before Caroline's death?

First, Gulyga notes that in 1803 there were rumors that Schelling was writing a novel. Although Gulyga hazards the theory that perhaps Schelling was writing *Die Nachtwachen* under the pseudonym of Bonaventura (this guess is also made in Tilliette 1981), *Clara* could also be a suitable candidate.[6] Indeed, it is now widely acknowledged that Schelling was not the author of *Die Nachtwachen*, thus leaving open the question of what novel it was that Schelling was working on.[7] If one couples the knowledge that Schelling was writing a novel with the facts I gave in the previous section—that Schelling was composing a second, highly symbolic discussion around 1804—*Clara* appears to be the only suitable candidate.

Second, it was at this time—just after the publication of *Bruno*—that there were public accusations that Schelling was responsible for the death of Auguste Böhmer. Auguste was the daughter from Caroline's first marriage. Schelling had been devastated by Auguste's death in 1800 and he hardly had the emotional energy to reply to the criticisms that were still being leveled against him. Therefore this outcry about his ostensible role in Auguste's death may have provoked Schelling to brood about life after death even this early—but in relation to Auguste rather than to Caroline—and to seek refuge in his writing.

Third, Tilliette (1970) notes that in a letter to Schubert dated 30 December 1808, Schelling wrote of clairvoyance as a foretaste of the future life. In this letter Schelling told Schubert that he, Schelling, perceived clairvoyance as a way of keeping what we have loved in the life beyond; for Schelling it was clairvoyance that would hold the key to how we can retain complete individuality within the dissolution into the whole at death. These thoughts echo those expressed in *Clara* and they were clearly present in Schelling's mind before he had any inkling that Caroline would die in September the following year. Schelling likewise indicated in this letter that he was writing a "literary" work and that he was dissatisfied because he had strayed too far from the central topic (presumably of clairvoyance and animal magnetism). Given the strong emphasis on clairvoyance in the sketch written on the back of the spring fragment, it does not seem unreasonable to hypothesize that the literary work to which Schelling refers was the *Clara* manuscript. We also know that, after writing the symbolic discussion that had the content of *Philosophie und Religion*, Schelling reordered his thoughts into what became *Of Human Freedom* in 1809. He may well have worked further on his symbolic discussion at this point also. Moreover, in a letter dated 15 November 1808, shortly before writing to Schubert about his literary work, Schelling mentioned to Cotta the oft-promised second "discussion." Thus, this second discussion was still in Schelling's mind just before he wrote to Schubert mentioning this literary work that never appeared. Indeed, if one takes the similarities between letters written shortly after Caroline's death and *Clara* as evidence that *Clara* was written in 1810, then surely the striking similarity already evident between Schelling's correspondence in 1808 and *Clara* should also be considered as evidence that some of *Clara* may have been written beforehand.

Finally, in the passage in *Clara* discussing an appropriate popular form for philosophy, Clara criticizes the difficult writing style of much of the current philosophy and wonders why philosophers don't write more for the people; the priest maintains that anything uniting philosophy and prose would be dismissed as a worthless half-breed. This section of *Clara* is generally acknowledged to be a critique of the very difficult prose in Hegel's *Phenomenology of Spirit* (Grau 1997, Kuhlenbeck 1913) and a reaction to Hegel's own protestations against the trivialization of philosophy (Gulyga 1989). For instance, in the preface to *Phenomenology*, Hegel wrote that "This latter [ignorance] was once just as rife in poetry as it is now in philosophy; but instead of poetry . . . it produced trivial prose or . . .

crazy discussions. So now a natural philosophizing ... brings to market ... works that are neither fish nor flesh, neither poetry nor philosophy" (Hegel 1807, 46; my translation). Schelling had received Hegel's *Phenomenology* to review in 1807, well before Caroline's death. Of course, Schelling need not have railed against this critique of an attempt to unify poetry and philosophy until later—indeed, after Caroline's death Schelling spent most of his life criticizing Hegel—but this section of *Clara* does leave the door open for the argument that Schelling's critique of Hegel in *Clara* was written in response to the initial break in Hegel and Schelling's relationship. Ehrhardt (forthcoming) offers a different view. He suggests that Clara's displeasure with philosophical prose is a reference to Krause's *Grundriß der historischen Logik* (1803). Ehrhardt reports that even Krause's biographer described the *Grundriß* as having been "written in the most repellent language." Ehrhardt additionally believes that when the priest says in this section that he and Clara discussed the philosophical novel "partly then, partly later" [92], Schelling is alluding to the numerous book reviews that he and Caroline published during 1805/6. These are just two reasons why Ehrhardt places the genesis of *Clara* at around 1803.

All four arguments outlined above serve to cast doubt on the current widely held assumption that *Clara* was written in its entirety in 1810; there are grounds to think that at least some of it was composed at an earlier date. However, these arguments need not provide any evidence for a connection of *Clara* to *Bruno*. *Bruno*, although a discussion, has a different aim and has no obvious link to the *Clara* manuscript.

Nevertheless, Schelling's son controversially dated *Clara* much later, at 1817. Although this estimate is generally regarded to be wrong, facts that could support this estimate are often ignored.

First, Tilliette (1977) notes that in 1817 Schelling was still fascinated by the possibility of paranormal phenomena: Schelling wrote to his brother in this year to ask him what he thought about action at a distance and about stories about spirits making knocking noises. In *Clara* there is a long discussion about whether spirits can exert an influence from their world to this one.

Second, as noted above, Schelling's son regarded it as unlikely that the whole of *Clara* was written by 1810 because its ideas on nature and the spirit world are more advanced than those in *The Ages of the World*. *Clara*, containing an account of a transition from the present to the future, has a different emphasis from the first book of *The Ages of the World*, which provides an account of the past to the present. This change in emphasis points to *Clara's* having been written later than the first book of *The Ages of the World*.

Third, Beckers (1865), like so many others, refers to the "Stuttgart Seminars" as a reason not to accept K. F. A. Schelling's view. The "Stuttgart Seminars" was written in 1810 and it too addresses the topic of the future life. But the "Stuttgart Seminars" is actually very different from *Clara*. True, there are a couple of analogies that appear in both works, but in terms of views and philosophical direction the two writings diverge quite strongly.

For instance, the "Stuttgart Seminars" focuses primarily on (1) the relationship between God and man, and (2) the Fall. These two themes reflect much more closely the content of the first book of *The Ages of the World* and of the *Freedom* essay, respectively, than that of *Clara*. Thus, given his interest in the Fall in the "Stuttgart Seminars," Schelling appropriately in that work discusses the contrast between heaven and hell, whereas the themes of the Fall and of heaven and hell play only a minor role in *Clara*. Instead of concerning himself with man's *original* Fall from God, in *Clara* Schelling emphasizes man as the *future* transitional point between nature and the spirit world. And in *Clara* the focus is on the need for *man* to enhance his internality in this life so that his transition to the next world will be easier; whereas in the "Stuttgart Seminars" man has to wait for *nature* to come into a crisis so that in nature, too, the principles are split and heaven and hell can finally order themselves in the appropriate way. The underlying metaphysics in both works is quite different.

A thorough discussion of the relationship between the "Stuttgart Seminars" and *Clara* is a crucial step toward a better understanding of Schelling's philosophical progress. This is not the place for such an enterprise, but I hope that my brief comments here are enough to show that Beckers is wrong to say without further justification that *Clara*'s content is reflected in the "Stuttgart Seminars"; it is not obvious that the two works are similar at all. Moreover, when laying down which works could be published after his death, Schelling dictated, regarding the "Stuttgart Seminars," that "only in the following years did I find the decisive ideas." Was it in *Clara* that Schelling found the decisive ideas? From the thoughts in this paragraph, it does not appear that *Clara* was completed as early as 1810. In 1810 Schelling is still preoccupied with the metaphysics from *Of Human Freedom*.

Fourth, Schelling continued to mourn Caroline for much longer than just the year immediately following her death. Even nine years after Caroline's death, when asked by Caroline's sister (Luise Wiedemann) if she could perhaps have Caroline's letters, Schelling replied to say that the memory of Caroline was still too painful for him to be able to look through the letters and place them in order. It is therefore possible that some of the passages apparently mourning Caroline's death could be a reawakened sorrow some number of years after the event. They do not have to have been written solely in 1810.

In sum, there are reasons to think that at least the germs of the ideas for *Clara* may have been formulated and written down before Caroline's death, but that the overall structure and concrete philosophical conceptualization of the text were settled after 1810. It is well known that after Caroline's death Schelling published very little. Instead, he rewrote everything many times over, never satisfied with what he had produced. There is no intrinsic reason to believe that Schelling did not go through this same process of continual rewriting with *Clara*. As Vetö (1973) notes, there were several versions of the *Clara* manuscript left behind after Schelling's death (Beckers 1865). This lends further support to the idea that *Clara* may not have a single year of composition. Indeed, Gulyga (1989) writes that

Schelling was finally happy with the content of his work, but not its form. Even toward the end of his life, Schelling wanted to provide a way of conveying his philosophical thoughts simply. It is clear that *Clara* was especially designed to be a popularly accessible piece of work and it may well be toward this type of work that Schelling was striving. Thus he may never have entirely abandoned *Clara*, but have always retained it at the back of his mind.

Nevertheless, I have not covered here the many reasons for placing *Clara* at 1810. If one has to date a manuscript, then 1810 is probably a good compromise, but it is essential to remember that it is only a compromise. Otherwise it is too easy to forget other possible links that *Clara* may forge within the corpus of Schelling's works. Although Vetö (1973) insightfully argues that *Clara* was written in early 1810—by citing a letter to Cotta on 13 March in which Schelling says he is busy writing and by referring to a letter to Schlegel written just the day before in which Schelling describes his current work as "unique"—most of the reasons for dating *Clara* at 1810 stem from an understanding of Schelling's personal circumstances. Because there is no biography of Schelling in English I will outline potentially important aspects of Schelling's life—and of those closest to him—in relation to *Clara*. Readers may then make their own assessments of the controversies that surround the genesis of the text. Although many of the parallels between *Clara* and Schelling's personal life provide compelling reasons for the dating of *Clara* at circa 1810, one must not become so blinded by these parallels that other possible connections are ignored. Schelling certainly had many of the ideas in his mind much earlier and he may even have composed the initial outline some time before 1810. Nevertheless, Schelling's biographical details are appropriate for an introduction to *Clara*, which was written for a wider audience. Indeed, Schelling's life itself reads like a novel.

SCHELLING—BIOGRAPHICAL DETAILS

Schelling's Early Years

Schelling's christening on 28 January 1775 was, by all accounts, quite an event for the small town of Leonberg in Baden-Württemberg with its thirteen hundred inhabitants. Eleven godparents are listed on the register and only two of these came from Leonberg (Schönwitz 1992). The christening took place just one day after his birth. Thus, as Schönwitz notes, those coming from outside of Leonberg had to have come at relatively short notice. At the time Schelling's father was the priest in Leonberg; he had published some well-received papers in theology and he was a highly regarded Orientalist also. Ironically, given Schelling's own later interest in the spirit world, Schelling's father had replaced Paulus in Leonberg because Paulus had been deemed to have an unacceptable interest in spirit seeing. The son, Heinrich Paulus, had been born in the same house fourteen years prior to Schelling, while the Paulus family was still there. Perhaps because of his father's history, Heinrich Paulus subsequently focused on rational theology, and, again ironically, when one thinks of the fate that befell his father, Paulus the younger later accused Schelling of obscurantism and mysticism, and of being unduly speculative.

Two years after Schelling's birth the family moved to Bebenhausen, where Schelling's father took a professorial post. In Bebenhausen, young "Fritz" Schelling learned to appreciate nature and the countryside; this love of nature would be reflected in his philosophy throughout his life (Gulyga 1989). He shone at school and began learning classical languages at the age of eight. When he was ten he went to a Latin school at Nürtingen, but returned to Bebenhausen at the age of twelve because there was nothing more the school could teach him. He took classes at his father's seminary alongside much older students and learned Oriental languages. Schelling's father was keen to promote his son's intellectual ability and gained special permission for Schelling to begin his university education early, at the nearby Tübinger Stift. Legally, university education could begin only at the age of eighteen, but even when just sixteen years old, Schelling shone at the Tübinger Stift. The three students who shared a room there—Hegel, Hölderlin, and Schelling—would each play a part in German intellectual history. At the Stift there was a lot of enthusiasm about the French Revolution; for the students the Revolution was a breath of fresh air in comparison with the stifling atmosphere of the university.

After Schelling finished at Tübingen, his father got him a position as a *Hauslehrer*—a private teacher—for a couple with adopted children. Becoming a private teacher was usually the first step after leaving university. The next step was to become a junior lecturer at a university (*Assistent*), then to write a *Habilitation* thesis (a postdoctoral qualification) in order to get a university position. Normally, one could aspire to a professorship only after completing a *Habilitation*. Schelling, however, had ambitions to become a professor straight away. His father, who was clearly ambitious for his son, supported this idea. Even though Schelling was only twenty-two in 1797, he had already published a number of works, including *On the Possibility of a Form of Philosophy in General*, *Philosophical Letters on Dogmatism and Criticism*, and *Ideas on a Philosophy of Nature*. His father was trying to obtain a professorship for him in Tübingen. Meanwhile, Heinrich Paulus—at that point still friendly with Schelling—and Fichte (among others) attempted to get Schelling a professorial post in Jena. The post in Jena was unpaid but in a more prestigious university, whereas the post at Tübingen would have been salaried. In a postscript to a letter to his father on 4 September 1797, Schelling expressed severe doubts that the position at Tübingen was a real possibility. He had higher hopes for the professorship at Jena. As it turned out, neither Tübingen nor Jena offered Schelling a professorial position in the first instance; Schelling informed his father on 30 March 1798 that Jena had offered him a position as *Privatdozent* (private lecturer) for six months and that they would thereafter promote him to a professorship. Schelling, however, found these terms quite unsatisfactory and turned the post down. The following year

Schelling published *On the World Soul*, which aroused Goethe's enthusiasm; Goethe subsequently wrote a letter recommending Schelling for the unpaid professorship at Jena. As a consequence, at the exceptionally young age of twenty-three, Schelling was called to the chair.

Schelling's new professorial life was to start in October. In the meantime August Wilhelm Schlegel invited Schelling to spend the summer with him, his wife Caroline, his brother Friedrich, and Friedrich von Hardenberg, better known as Novalis. At first Schelling lived with the Niethammers, but he later moved into August Wilhelm and Caroline Schlegel's house. Friedrich Schlegel, Dorothea Veit, and Ludwig Tieck were all to move to Jena, with Novalis also visiting. This became known as the Jena circle, the melting pot for the Romantic movement.

It was in these first few years in Jena that the critical relationship between Schelling, Caroline, and Auguste developed. And it is these years that are possibly the most relevant for understanding the *Clara* manuscript.

CAROLINE—BACKGROUND

At the time that Schelling moved into the Schlegel's household, Caroline was married to August Wilhelm and had a child, Auguste, from her first marriage. The relationship between Schelling, Auguste, and Caroline is in places ambiguous and in the end fateful. To understand the factors at play, we need to look at the time before Caroline was married to Wilhelm.

Caroline was the daughter of the famous Orientalist, Michaelis. She was christened Dorothea Caroline Albertine in September 1763 and she had two sisters, a brother, and a half-brother. As a child she caught chicken pox, which left marks on her face; as a result she was the least pretty of the daughters. Her grandmother consequently left money in her will to provide Caroline with an education so that her learning would make her a more eligible wife. Caroline's first marriage was arranged by her parents—this was quite the usual practice at that time. The husband they chose for her was her next-door neighbor, the doctor Johann Böhmer. He was Caroline's elder by ten years. Caroline gave birth to their first child, Auguste, in April 1785. The birth was difficult; Caroline's health had never been good, but both mother and daughter survived. The child was sometimes called Gustel or Uttelchen for short.[8] A second daughter, Therese, followed, but two months later Böhmer died, leaving Caroline alone with two children. Therese died just over two years later, leaving Caroline with only Auguste. In 1792 Mainz was taken by the French and, like Schelling and the others in Tübingen, Caroline was initially enthusiastic about the revolution.

Her childhood friend, Therese Heyne, had married Georg Forster, who headed the revolutionary movement in Mainz. However, Therese left Forster for a married man and Caroline was left to comfort Forster. Rumors abounded that Caroline and Forster had had an affair and that Caroline was the reason for the breakup of the marriage. Although this was untrue, Therese Heyne helped spread the rumors in order to protect herself. Forster eventually left to go to France. Caroline was finally persuaded to leave Mainz. However, as she tried to leave, she and Auguste were arrested by the Prussians, who mistakenly thought that she was Georg Böhmer's wife. Georg Böhmer was her late husband's brother and headed the revolutionary Jacobins in Mainz. The Prussians had also heard and believed the rumors about her being Forster's lover. As a result, she and Auguste were thrown into prison. While there Caroline found to her dismay that she was pregnant from a brief relationship she had had with a French lieutenant. This was a disaster for her. If she bore a child outside of wedlock, she would be deemed an unfit mother and her beloved daughter Auguste could be taken away from her. Moreover, the father of the unborn child was a French soldier—an "enemy"—there would be no hope of either Caroline or Auguste ever coming out of prison. In particular, Auguste's life would not be worth living with such a tarnished background. Caroline was terrified of losing Auguste and even contemplated suicide to protect Auguste from the potential scandal.

Eventually Caroline's youngest brother helped her get out of prison. In order to go into hiding without raising too much curiosity, she told people she wanted to live quietly for a while after the trauma of having been in prison (Ritchie 1968). It was at this point that the Schlegel brothers played an important role in her life. Wilhelm Schlegel had courted Caroline four years earlier, but Caroline had turned him down. The relationship between Caroline and Friedrich Schlegel is a little more ambiguous; it is generally thought that he, too, was in love with Caroline but that he recognized his older brother as having the first claim on her. The Schlegel brothers arranged for Caroline to go into hiding until she gave birth to the child, and they helped keep her secret from being discovered. She named the child Wilhelm Julius. He was given to foster parents, but he died early, aged only seventeen months. Because the child had been born in secret, Caroline was unable to show her distress to the outside world. In 1796 Caroline finally agreed to marry Wilhelm Schlegel, after pressure from her parents. The marriage for Caroline did not grow out of love, but out of a necessity to give Auguste and herself a protector, and out of her feeling of thankfulness for all that Wilhelm had done for them. Indeed, Caroline was still tarnished by her involvement in the revolution; she was even forbidden to live in some cities in Germany. Her marriage to Schlegel helped her overcome these stains on her character and lead a freer life. The marriage was an "open" one; even if Wilhelm really did love Caroline, he nevertheless had many mistresses. Through the Schlegels Caroline circulated among the leading figures of the Romantic movement.

While Caroline was married to Wilhelm, Schelling began his unpaid professorial position in Jena, living in the Schlegels' house and in 1799 eating regularly with them. How did the story develop from there?

Schelling and Auguste

There is no clear picture of what relations were originally like between Caroline, Schelling, and Auguste. In 1799, Auguste was a relatively mature thirteen year old, Schelling was twenty-four and Caroline was thirty-six. Some biographers claim that Schelling was originally interested in Auguste, but that Auguste did not show any interest (Gulyga 1989). Apart from Dorothea Veit's rumormongering to this effect, there appears to be little evidence for this view, although Schelling clearly tried his best to smooth relations between himself and Auguste. Friedrich Schlegel wrote to Caroline, "I admire Schelling for sending Auguste flowers. I hope I will be there next time he does it." It is impossible to know whether this gift of flowers was merely an attempt to smooth relations between him and Auguste or whether some deeper emotion was attached to it. Others claim that Caroline was immediately attracted to Schelling (Gulyga 1989), but, realizing that it was impossible to have a relationship with him because of her marriage to Wilhelm, she encouraged a relationship between Auguste and Schelling in order to keep Schelling near her. Yet others maintain that the only reason for thinking that there was anything between Schelling and Auguste is due to rumors initiated by Dorothea Veit, Friedrich Schlegel's wife, because Friedrich was upset at seeing his brother's marital difficulties (Kleßmann 1975).

What is for certain is that relations were initially cool between Schelling and Auguste. Caroline often wrote that Auguste's manners to Schelling were not what they could be. In September 1799 Caroline sent Auguste to friends in Dessau to further her education, and Caroline and Schelling became closer. Auguste's letters at this time clearly indicate that she was not happy at being separated from her mother for such a long time. One passage from a letter in this period from Caroline to Auguste is cited by many commentators with a variety of interpretations. In the letter, Caroline reprimanded Auguste with the following words: "What you said last time against Schelling wasn't very nice at all. If you battle so much against him, I'll start to think you are jealous of your mother" (14 October 1799). Some have read this passage as Caroline's finally admitting her own passion for Schelling; others claim that it was Auguste who was the jealous one. Schelling was taking up Caroline's attention and Auguste felt she was being shut out of her mother's life (Kahn-Wallenstein 1959). It could also be read as an indication that Auguste and Caroline were rivals for Schelling's attentions, with Caroline gloating to her daughter that she now had Schelling's favor. Which interpretation is the most likely?

In the light of the earlier letters in which Auguste complained bitterly about having to be so far away from her mother, Auguste does indeed appear to have been jealous of all the time her mother was spending with Schelling. However, if the cited passage is seen in context, Auguste's complaint was in response to something her mother had previously written. Namely, in the last letter she had received from her mother (30 September 1799), Auguste thought that Schelling had told her not to come back behaving like an "immature and stubborn little madam." However, in the October letter to Auguste cited above, Caroline corrected this view and said that those words were from her, Caroline, and not from Schelling. Thus, the interpretation that the jealousy was Auguste's appears wrong in this instance. Auguste was protesting against what she perceived to be an insult. Thus, Caroline's interpretation of Auguste's reaction as jealousy is more likely to be a spontaneous confession as to her (Caroline's) own emotions regarding Schelling. Also, the previous harsh words to Auguste from Caroline indicate that Caroline was now letting Auguste know very clearly that Schelling was going to play an important part in her (Caroline's) life and that Auguste would have to adapt to it. From about this point onwards, Schelling and Auguste came to be on better terms and Auguste even made jokes about the availability of Schelling's brother (see the letter from Caroline to Auguste, 21 October 1799).

Those around the Schlegels soon realized that the marriage between Wilhelm and Caroline was not going well, and Friedrich Schlegel, Dorothea Veit, and Tieck all refused to speak to Schelling. Relations between Wilhelm Schlegel and Schelling nevertheless remained surprisingly good. However, whenever there were emotional pressures Caroline often become unwell. With all the animosity around her regarding her relationship to Schelling, and with her wanting to be with Schelling, in March 1800 Caroline fell seriously ill. Hufeland was the practicing doctor; Schelling was unhappy with Hufeland's treatment of Caroline and insisted on intervening with his own prescriptions. Schelling wanted Hufeland to use a Brownian method to treat the rapidly ailing Caroline.

John Brown (1735-1788) held in his *Elementa Medicinae* that life is sustained through stimuli to which the organism reacts by means of its arousability. If the body is too strongly or weakly aroused or if the stimuli are likewise too strong or weak, illness arises. Asthenic illnesses were caused by too weak an arousal and had to be treated by stimulants; sthenic maladies arose from too strong an arousal and had to be treated with sedatives (Gerabek 1995, 85). As a method that applied to all illnesses, Brown's theory was taken up eagerly by the Romantics and reinterpreted by Röschlaub, even though it met much controversy on its home ground (Scotland/England). Schelling was attracted to Brown's method due to its basis in the theory that the body tries to unite two opposing factors without stepping outside of the opposition. This was, of course, in accord with Schelling's philosophical views in general.

After hearing of Schelling's prescriptions, Goethe sent some Hungarian wine to help treat Caroline, which, Wilhelm Schlegel said, "worked as a true balsam." Schelling's intervention using wine, Chinin, opium, and nutritive creams, among other things, was successful and Caroline recovered.

When Auguste writes about these events to Luise Gotter, a friend of her mother's, Auguste makes no mention of Schelling's role in Caroline's recovery. Kahn-Wallenstein (1959) postulates that Auguste's failure to mention Schelling quite generally in her letters to others stems from Caroline's not wanting rumors to spread too far. That is, Caroline has given Auguste strict instructions not to mention Schelling. Nevertheless, even in describing Caroline's close escape from death, Auguste does not mention Schelling once. She relates:

> Mother really has been very ill and still has not completely recovered. First she got a nervous fever which was very bad for eight days, then the doctor ordered a mustard plaster on her leg, this stayed on for too

long and was followed by an inappropriate ointment, so that it became very bad and caused mother great pain. This put her back so much that she got the nervous fever again, and now that it is over, she still has very strong cramps which are now beginning to diminish and each day we see her get better. It was said that a few times her life was in danger, but this is too terrible a thought for me to have.

Friedrich Schlegel, however, who by this point strongly disapproved of Schelling because he saw him as responsible for the breakup of Wilhelm and Caroline's marriage, did not hesitate to praise Schelling's role in saving Caroline's life. He wrote to Schleiermacher:

> I have now had the opportunity to learn about the Brownian method and since I have no further revelations about it I must content myself with worshipping the wonder that it brought about. At the beginning Hufeland treated Caroline against the Brownian prescriptions and she rapidly deteriorated; Schelling, however, pestered H. so much that finally he gave in and prescribed her stimulants and continual applications of Hungarian wine, nutritive creams . . . And wonders happened before our eyes.

In order to recuperate fully, Caroline went to Bad Bocklet in June 1800 with Auguste. Schelling joined them at the beginning of July. Wilhelm Schlegel was not present. However, just as Caroline was getting better, Auguste fell ill with dysentery. Presumably encouraged by his success in curing Caroline, Schelling again did not trust the doctors and he insisted on intervening in their prescriptions for Auguste. However, this time Schelling's intervention failed and on 12 July Caroline's only remaining child died. Auguste was only fifteen years old.

Schelling and Caroline

Wilhelm, Caroline, and Schelling were devastated at the loss of Auguste. Back in Jena, all those who disapproved of Caroline and Schelling's relationship were quick to place the blame for Auguste's death squarely on Schelling. His beneficial role in Caroline's recovery was now completely forgotten. Indeed, in those days the death of the daughter while the mother had gone away with her lover was interpreted as a warning from God. Both Schelling and Caroline had reasons to recriminate themselves.

Caroline's thoughts afterwards were completely with Auguste and she would never fully recover from this shock. In January Caroline wrote to Schelling:

> If the clouds of my sorrow cover even my head for a while, my head is soon clear again and is shone upon by the pure blue of the heavens above me that contain my child as well as me. This omnipresence is the

divinity—and don't you think that one day we must all become omnipresent, all one in the other, without thereby becoming one?

A similar passage can be found in *Clara* when the priest says:

> Only I don't quite see, I continued, that it necessarily follows that we would lose our particular existence if we came completely one with the divine. For the drop in the ocean nevertheless always is this drop even if it isn't distinguished as such. . . . Thus if we also imagine that at death the pious would be enraptured by God in a blessed delight as if by a universal magnet to which everything is attracted, such that they would now be completely suffused by Him and would see, feel, and want only within Him, then I don't see why their whole individuality would thereby be lost at the same time.

Just as Caroline became suffused by the thought of Auguste, so, too, is *Clara* as a work of mourning itself suffused with Auguste's presence.

Wilhelm, Caroline, and Schelling eventually had to resume a semblance of life and Wilhelm took Caroline back to Brunswick. Schelling became ill and severely depressed and returned to Jena. Despite her grief, Caroline was concerned for Schelling and asked Goethe to invite Schelling to spend Christmas with him. The invitation was promptly sent to Schelling and Schelling accepted. Caroline and Schelling remained in correspondence throughout the following months.

Initially the shared pain in Auguste's death seemed to bring Schelling and Caroline closer together. Schelling gave Caroline a ring that was intended to symbolize their engagement, even if this was not possible due to Caroline's marriage to Wilhelm. Caroline responded to Schelling in the following way, having explained that she was not emotionally able to meet him to give him a ring from her: "It is the pure gold of your pain that I recognize and that I exchange with mine. But there is some pain that I must hold back and that can only ever be mine."

Auguste's death was weighing heavily on Caroline's mind. Nevertheless, Caroline was still in love with Schelling and she told him that she had been trying hard to imagine what he was doing at Goethe's over Christmas. But other people's recriminations as to her role in what had happened took their toll and a month later she could not cope with the guilt that Auguste's death was perhaps some kind of divine retribution. In February she explained to Schelling: "If you blame yourself, then I blame myself a thousand times more. . . . I loved you, it was not a cruel game and that absolves me, I hope."

But she clearly did not feel absolved and to make amends she turned her relationship with Schelling into one of friendship rather than of romantic love. Thus in the same letter she wrote: "I greet you as your mother, no memory shall destroy us. You are my child's brother, I give you this holy blessing."

Schelling was shaken and devastated and could not accept what Caroline was telling him. But Caroline did her best to make amends with Wilhelm and to be a good wife. Relations between Caroline and Wilhelm improved and they appeared to return to a relatively happy marriage once more.

Schelling tried to forget his troubles through his work. In January he published "On the True Concept of Natural Philosophy," and later that year he referred to his work as a system for the first time. Wilhelm Schlegel also published four poems by Schelling in 1802, written under the pseudonym of Bonaventura. It was at this point in his life that Schelling most experimented with various literary forms. In addition to the poems, he published his *Presentation of My Philosophical System*, written in a manner similar to that of Spinoza, and then he followed this with *Bruno*, written in the style of a Platonic dialogue. A dialogue by Schelling also appeared in the *Kritisches Journal* in 1802. However, this was not the only period in which Schelling used different literary forms. His poem "Epikurische Glaubensbekenntnisse Heinz Widersportens" was written before Auguste's death in 1799 and his first published work was a poem.

But let us return to 1801. Despite Caroline's attempt to return to Wilhelm, their relationship gradually deteriorated again. Caroline spent more time with Schelling and they drew ever closer. But while Caroline and Wilhelm's marriage was falling apart, Schütz published an anonymous article in his *Allgemeine Literaturzeitung* in 1802 that accused Schelling of having murdered Auguste. Devastated, Schelling turned to Wilhelm Schlegel for help. Wilhelm and Caroline's crumbling marriage appears not to have affected the relations between Wilhelm and Schelling. Indeed, Wilhelm wrote to the *Allgemeine Literaturzeitung* demanding that they retract their libelous statements against Schelling. Instead, the paper just repeated the accusation, but in milder terms; Schelling was still held by them as ultimately responsible for Auguste's death. In the end Schelling suggested that Schlegel leave the matter and that he himself would reply when he had the energy. But Schelling never did and he appeared to stop producing any work for some time.

Wilhelm and Caroline's marriage was annulled in May 1803. Shortly afterward, in July, Schelling and Caroline were married by Schelling's father. The couple honeymooned in Cannstadt and visited the places of Schelling's youth, including Tübingen.

There was a further war and Würzburg fell to Bavaria, resulting in Schelling's being called to a paid professorship in Würzburg. However, Schütz, who had published the libelous statements about Schelling's role in Auguste's death, had also been called to a professorship and Schelling refused to take up his post if Schütz was going to be there. He won this battle; Schütz was not called to Würzburg and Schelling took up his professorship amid opposition from Paulus, who had suggested that Eschenmayer should have the post. At about this time Paulus wrote to Niethammer (17 November 1803) that Schelling was composing a novel; in terms of other publications Schelling was relatively quiet. Like so many of Schelling's projects that he announced, this novel never saw the light of day. He published *Philosophy and Religion* in early 1804, which he wrote in just eight days. In this year Schelling was yet again publicly attacked for being responsible for Auguste's death.

In 1805 another war meant that Würzburg fell to Austria. All Protestant professors had to quit their positions; this included Schelling. He decided to move to Munich, but he had no professorial position.

It was at this point that Schelling became very interested in occult phenomena. With Ritter, he conducted and published some experiments on an Italian dowser named Campetti. Campetti was later discovered to be a fraud, but Schelling's interests went beyond Campetti. Schelling started to read Böhme and he theorized about clairvoyance. It was also around this time (1806) that Schelling promised Cotta that he would publish some philosophical discussions and a work on methodology. Neither appeared.

In 1807, Hegel sent Schelling his *Phenomenology of Spirit* and asked Schelling to review it. In this work, Hegel criticized what he felt were Schelling's empty applications of formulae and he expressed the opinion that any attempt to unify philosophy and poetry would lead to trivial prose. It was from this point that relations between Hegel and Schelling began to fade.

The following year Schelling was given the honor of setting up and heading the Bavarian Academy of Arts by the crown prince who had been much impressed by a lecture that Schelling gave on the relationship of the pictorial arts to nature. This lecture had received much applause.

Schelling's letters from 1806 to 1808 often speculate about clairvoyance, dowsing, and animal magnetism. His brother Karl was actively engaged in animal magnetism and was excited about a patient of his who had apparently foreseen a death. The two brothers corresponded about this patient, with Schelling offering helpful comments. Karl Schelling later published this study. In 1807 Windischmann brought out a book of discussions on rebirth; Schelling told Windischmann that the book should have laid greater emphasis on the role of the will, and he speculated that our muscles could be compared to dowsing rods. Another friend, Schubert, wrote to Schelling with details of his lectures on oracles, animal magnetism, and the planets. In a letter to Schubert in 1808 Schelling hypothesized that clairvoyance is a

> foretaste of our future existence, or better, an inversion . . . the path to a complete conservation in the beyond of what we have loved, of our life from its beginning right up to its supposed end, without necessitating the organs and means that we are used to having accompany our individuality, in short the mystery of complete individuality with a complete dissolution into the one and the whole.

As Tilliette (1970) notes, this passage is very similar to the thoughts presented in *Clara*, even though it was written two years before the time most people believe *Clara* was written.

The following year Schelling became ill, but recovered. Later that year, in August, Caroline and Schelling visited Schelling's parents in Maulbronn; Schelling was tired after the journey. When he was better, he and Caroline went for a three-day hike. Upon their return, Caroline fell ill. At first it was not thought to be a serious illness, but her fever got worse and she died on 7 September.

Schelling was distraught and at first appeared obsessed with the idea that Caroline knew that she was going to die. On writing to Luise Gotter, Caroline's best friend, he noted that "[At dinner] her first words were: Schelling, if [*wenn*] I come back, I think I would like to have a different apartment after all. I took her to mean 'when' [*quand*]."

In German the word "*wenn*" can translate as either "if" or "when." So, on hearing these words the first time, Schelling assumed that Caroline meant "when"; but, looking back, he wondered if Caroline was already expressing doubt about whether she would return. Later in the same letter Schelling wrote: "Once, looking through the window at Maulbronn, she said to me: Schelling, do you think I could die here.... But it was I who was ill, she was the healthy one!"

He began an exchange of letters with Pauline Gotter—one of Luise Gotter's daughters. This correspondence lasted some years. The two of them were drawn together through their mutual suffering over the death of Caroline. Indeed, at least at the very beginning of the correspondence, various relationships seemed to get intermingled. For Schelling, writing to Pauline Gotter was like having a direct connection to his deceased wife. He told her on 9 October 1809: "She [Caroline] was so good to you and was recently involved with you so much, that words that come from you are almost as if they come from *her*."

At this time Pauline was also in close contact with Goethe, who had just written *Die Wahlverwandschaften* (*The Elective Affinities*), a work that was supposedly inspired by Caroline and Schelling's relationship. Schelling was curious about this work and asked Pauline if she knew anything about it.

Four months later Schelling was still mourning Caroline and he wrote to Pauline that "now that my dear one is no longer, it is as if only now have I also completely lost Auguste."

In the same letter (12 February 1810) he wrote:

> Let him [Schelling] often hear the gentle tones of your voice—(does Pauline *sing* too?)—and help him fully to gain the composure that's worthy of the holy feeling that must remain with him eternally, that can go over into sweet pain but that can never stop being pain.

This reference to the tones of Pauline's voice is reminiscent of his description of Caroline's melodious tones on her deathbed, her voice that always had been beautiful (see below). Thus, initially, writing to Pauline made Schelling feel closer to Caroline; Pauline even seemed to merge into Caroline. In turn, the death and memories of Caroline brought back memories of, and was strongly connected with, the death of Auguste. Indeed, Auguste too liked to sing more than anything else. The three women—Pauline, Caroline, and Auguste—became tightly intermingled in Schelling's mind. Schelling's correspondence with Pauline continued.

Schelling's Letters and Their Similarity to Clara

Much of the content of Schelling's letters written just after Caroline's death reappears in *Clara*. For instance, in describing Caroline's last moments to Luise Gotter, Schelling wrote:

> During the last evening she [Caroline] felt happy and better; the whole beauty of her lovely soul opened out again, her voice, which always had been beautiful, became music.

Similarly, in *Clara*, Clara exclaims:

> You remind me of my friend . . . how, as the shadow of death was approaching, a heavenly transfiguration shone within her whole being and that I believed never to have seen her so beautiful as in that moment approaching her demise . . . ; how her voice which always had a melodic sound then became heavenly music. [66]

Aspects from this passage in *Clara* are likewise to be found later in the same letter when Schelling explained to Luise Gotter that

> when she died, she lay with the sweetest inclination of her head, with an expression on her face of happiness and of the most wonderful peace.

These descriptions of Caroline's death seem to have come from *Clara* or vice versa. Just as Caroline looked wonderful on her deathbed, so too does Clara's friend as she dies.[9]

Even Schelling's worldview at this time is echoed both in his letters and in *Clara*. For instance, he exclaimed in this same letter to Luise Gotter:

> What a terrible circle of fateful connections is closed through this death! Nine years ago the same illness took away the lovely daughter as she was away from home; now also when away from home it takes away the precious life of the mother. But now *she* is happy; her heart had largely already been on the other side for some time.

This idea of strange connections over time persisted and on 27 May 1810 he was prompted to comment to Pauline: "She [Caroline] often told me how her grandfather said: he had outlived *her!*—How sweet is the thought that in a harmonious world we must expect to find the same or the similar according to the internal law of relationships."

Here Schelling noted that he had outlived Caroline just as Caroline's grandfather had outlived his wife. This idea of an "internal law of relationships" is present in *Clara* too. For example, in the section immediately following the introduction the characters are struck by the similarity between one of the pictures of Clara's forebears and Clara herself; in the discussion at Christmas, Clara remarks on the likeness between the priest's daughter and her (the daughter's) late mother. It causes Clara to speculate that the mother is around and watching over them. Moreover, Clara's thoughts, too, are often "on the other side."

Caroline's presence can be felt in many passages. Clara says, for instance:

> If children had been given to me and then they were all taken away, I could never consider it as chance or a temporary fortune to have been the mother of these souls; I would feel, even know, that they belong to me eternally and I to them and that no power in earth or heaven could take them from me or me from them. [19]

This description fit Caroline very well. All her children had been taken away by death. She felt as if she retained some connection to Auguste even after Auguste's death. Schelling too felt that Caroline would remain his, just as Clara felt that a mother's children belong eternally to the mother. The parallels are striking.

Some of Pauline's thoughts written to Schelling are—perhaps coincidentally—likewise echoed in *Clara*. She related to Schelling on 17 June 1810:

> We are living quietly and studiously in an almost monastic lonesomeness . . . and when we climb through the ruins of the old castle in the evening and my eye, losing itself in the blue distance, seeks out the areas where my departed friends live, the memory of them swells up in me twice as much.

In the first section of *Clara* the priest relates the following incident:

> The direction of her eyes drew me toward the open window, and as she caught sight of the blue and remote hills, her eyes filled with tears and she said: Behind those hills yonder which will become bluer and bluer and over which the sun is now about to sink, there lies buried everything *I* have. Oh Albert, Albert, we had to leave the quiet sanctuary that united us on this side, only to be separated for so long—oh who knows how long. [15]

Thus, just as Pauline was caused to think of her departed friends when she looked into the blue distance, Clara's thoughts, too, turn more strongly to her beloved Albert when she sees the remote blue hills.

Philosophically, Schelling retained the ideas he had earlier that personality remains after death. Thus at Easter 1811 Schelling wrote to Georgii on hearing about the death of the latter's wife:

> We can't be satisfied with a general survival of the deceased, we require that their whole personality be retained and not to lose from them even one small detail.

This echoes passages in *Clara* such as the following:

> Rather I would have thought that although body and spirit may undergo many changes, what had been myself from the very beginning, what seemed to me and to others to remain always the same . . . would always remain the same . . . I understand it as meaning that what would live eternally would be just that innermost being, my own self. [47–48]

Later on in this letter to Georgii, Schelling remarked:

> Even death, which may cause us to curse our dependence on nature and which fills a human soul's first impression almost with horror against this merciless violence, and which destroys even the most beautiful and best without mercy when her laws demand it, even death, when grasped more deeply, opens up our eyes to the unity of the natural and the divine.

This is comparable to the doctor's remarks in *Clara*:

> As humans we may like to complain about the downfall of the most beautiful and lovely things in the world; but at the same time we should consider each such Fall with a kind of quiet joy, because it holds a confirmation of the view that we must have of this world and it is our most immediate reference to another, higher world. [37]

Clearly, the borders between Schelling's personal life and his philosophy dissolve at this point.

The descriptions of the characters in *Clara* seem to be taken at least partly from life. Thus Schelling informs Pauline on 30 January 1811 that "I now live in such isolation that, apart from a daily walk, I don't go out of the house and I don't see anyone apart from a young friend who is a keen zoologist and natural scientist who is my house and table companion."

Likewise in *Clara*, Clara is portrayed as living alone in her house and the only people she sees are a natural scientist (the doctor) and the priest. The similarities are striking. The young friend to whom Schelling refers was probably J. B. Spix.[10] If Spix did not come to Munich until 1811 and Schelling is drawing on his personal circumstances in composing *Clara*, this passage might speak against *Clara*'s having been completed by 1810.

Immediately after Caroline's death, Schelling could not bear to live in Munich, where there were too many memories of Caroline, so he moved temporarily to Stuttgart. In 1810 he gave some private lectures at a popular level to a small audience in which he discussed, among other things, life after death. These are known as the "Stuttgart Seminars."

The "Stuttgart Seminars" were informal and, though written down, were never published in Schelling's lifetime. Indeed, after Caroline's death Schelling published very little. This does not mean he was unproductive. He wrote—and continually rewrote—three of his major works, namely: *Philosophy of Mythology*, *Philosophy of Revelation*, and *The Ages of the World*. But he could never quite bring them to print, each time insisting on a last few corrections.

Almost a year to the day after Caroline died, Schelling's sister's child, whom he adored, also died at Maulbronn and from the very same illness that Caroline had had. Again, Pauline was a sympathetic correspondent to whom he could turn.

Schelling and Pauline

It is possible to read Pauline's letters as cautious advances to Schelling. At first Schelling and Pauline acknowledged each other as one of only a few people with whom they could really share their grief over Caroline's death. The information that Pauline gave Schelling was bound to arouse his sympathy. She had a love of children, and she wrote on 17 June 1810 of the nephew of Ziegesar: "The lovely child loves me so much that it doesn't leave my side and even I do not have the heart to leave it, when it stretches out its little tiny arms to me and calls in its gentle voice: Pauline-y, Pauline-y."

Pauline also saw Goethe frequently, which raised Schelling's interest. Similarly, she shared Schelling's love of the countryside. The relationship between Schelling and Pauline slowly developed. In the letter of 8 November Pauline made the first cautious, indirect suggestion that she and Schelling should see each other. She wrote, "We meet so many people in life to whom we are indifferent, why is fate seldom so kind as to bring us together with those whom we love and respect. So I fear, dear Schelling, we will never see each other again."

In spring, her letters to Schelling became more affectionate. On 16 March 1811 she now put Schelling first, before mentioning Caroline: "I can say that with the first cheering sight of sunshine, my thoughts were with you, dear Schelling! But not forgetting the loved one whom you miss with each beautiful joy."

Later in this letter she wrote of her somewhat flirtatious relationship to Goethe and enclosed Goethe's poem "Action at a distance" with her letter, closing the correspondence with the following lines: "Fare well, dearest Schelling. Write soon, for a note from the hand of a dear friend nevertheless remains the *truest* action at a distance."

It is almost as if Pauline was saying that although she was flirting with Goethe, her real interest was in Schelling. Three days later Schelling wrote to Georgii: "Daily I come to recognize more that everything is connected much more personally and intensely than we care to imagine."

It is possible that Schelling was starting to see Pauline as more than a friend, and that the talk of "action at a distance" reinforced in his head the connection he originally had made between Pauline and Caroline. Perhaps it was as if Caroline was speaking through Pauline. Pauline was tactful enough to still acknowledge Schelling's love for Caroline in her letters. Schelling reciprocated Pauline's affection and in June he replied, "Today I am alone, but I have lightened up my loneliness by writing to you. Please me again soon with a line from your hand. I think you must feel how often and how much I am with you; after all I foresaw that you had written to me! If your feelings likewise travel into the distance, then over the last few days you must have quite involuntarily thought of me a lot."

They finally arranged to meet in May 1812. In reality, the meeting was to determine whether they would make suitable marriage partners. Pauline brought her mother and sisters; Schelling brought his friend Marcus for a doctor's opinion on Pauline's health. He did not want to have to suffer another early death of a loved one. Schelling and Pauline were both pleased with what they saw, and in June, just one month later, they married.

Pauline soon became pregnant. However, just four months after they married, a letter arrived announcing that Schelling's father had died. Pauline had a miscarriage and Schelling feared that they would not be able to have children. However, in December of the following year Pauline gave birth to their first son, Paul (after Pauline), much to Schelling's delight. In 1815 Friedrich (after Schelling, presumably) was born. Their first two daughters were named, rather astonishingly, Caroline (in 1817) and Clara (in 1818). Does this mean that Schelling was still thinking about the *Clara* manuscript even at this stage? In 1821 their third daughter, Julia, was born. Their sixth and last child, Hermann, was born in 1824. By this time Schelling was forty-nine.

Hegel died in 1831, but his philosophy continued to be influential. He had gained the reputation of being Germany's foremost philosopher, but Schelling actually had the more influential position. In 1840, at the age of sixty-five, Schelling was called to Berlin to take Hegel's chair. It was a big move for Schelling to go from Munich all the way to Berlin at his age, especially after spending so many settled years in Munich, but the post held the attraction of enabling him possibly to convert some Hegelians to his own philosophy. After much deliberation, Schelling decided to take up the offer. He stopped lecturing in 1846, although his lectures were as popular as ever and the students asked him to continue. In 1853 Schelling's health deteriorated. He made a list of contents of his work and gave his son Karl Friedrich the responsibility of producing his collected works after his death.

Schelling died in 1854 at the age of seventy-nine in Bad Ragaz, Switzerland. He thus fulfilled his wish, expressed to Pauline in 1818, that "even more intensely than what is now almost four years ago, I wish I could live with you for a whole 40 years." From Schelling's calculations in this letter he did indeed live exactly forty years with Pauline, for he died thirty-six years after writing this letter.[11] He was buried in Bad Ragaz and the Bavarian king erected a monument there in his memory, with the title "To the first thinker of Germany." Pauline followed him to the grave less than four months later, on 13 December. Karl Friedrich lived just long enough to bring out the collected works and the first single edition of *Clara*; then he died in 1864, just ten years after his father.

WHO IS CLARA?

Because of Schelling's colorful life and extensive knowledge, accounts differ widely as to why Schelling chose the name "Clara" for one of the central characters in the discussion. Some commentators write as if there is absolutely no controversy; others are more cautious. I will describe the main views below.

In the text the priest generally argues for the spiritual; the doctor represents arguments in favor of nature, the material, and the corporeal; and Clara embodies the soul or personality. It is thus fitting that Clara is the only main character in the discussions who is given a name. She is also the only one whose character is developed. For Schelling's philosophy, of course, it is important that all three characters interact and that each takes a turn at leading the discussion. That is, the structure of the discussions as well as the representations of the interlocutors are themselves part and parcel of the philosophical meaning of the entire text.

However, there are two minor characters in the text who are also given names—Albert, Clara's deceased loved one, and Therese, one of the priest's children. It may be of interest to ask why these characters, too, were given names. Perhaps it is relevant that one of Caroline's middle names was 'Albertine' and that her second child was called 'Therese.' Ehrhardt (forthcoming) argues that Albert represents Auguste. In support of this view he cites a letter dated 17 September 1803 from Caroline to her sister Luise. In this letter Caroline refers to "a holy ground where Auguste rests and which, a half-day's journey from Würzburg, I saw with pain in someone else's possession." Ehrhardt notes that this passage is strikingly similar to Clara's looking out the window to where everything she has (i.e., Albert) is buried.

One of the more popular beliefs surrounding Schelling's choice of the name "Clara" is that Clara is supposed to represent Caroline. The names are similar and given that at least some passages in the text were clearly written shortly after Caroline's death, it is possible that the discussions were written in part to immortalize his recently deceased wife. The character is mourning the death of her loved one, Albert, and struggles to overcome this grief. Similarly, Caroline never really recovered from the death of Auguste. Indeed, Schelling wrote after Caroline's death that part of her spirit had already been on the other side for a long time, and this is precisely what Clara expresses in the text. Horn (1997) argues that perhaps Schelling chose the name "Clara" because Goethe had once described Caroline as "camera clara." I find this a bit far-fetched.

Another possible reason might stem from the fact that Schelling avidly read all of Caroline's former correspondence after she died, asking various people if they could loan him any letters they had from her. If he also re-read the letters that she wrote to him shortly after Auguste's death, he may have been struck by the one in which Caroline wrote, "The blue coat wrapped you like Count Egmont. Oh that I could be your little Clara [Clärchen], but I am only your Caroline."

Egmont is a play by Goethe and Clärchen is Egmont's loved one. Thus, *Clara* may be Schelling's attempt to fulfill the wish Caroline had of becoming his own Clara.

A more sophisticated version of the above view is that Schelling is speaking as Clara. That is, Clara represents Schelling, but Schelling is speaking through a character that is named after Caroline. This is supported, among other ways, by Clara's uttering many sentences that Schelling himself wrote to those close to him after Caroline's death. In this case, then, Albert represents Caroline, whom Schelling is mourning through the character of Clara. Indeed, Albertine was one of Caroline's middle names. Nevertheless, even in this view "Clara" was essentially chosen as a name because of Caroline.

A different view is that Clara is Pauline, as the character expresses some sorrows that Pauline expressed at the death of Caroline. Nevertheless, this is not particularly convincing as a reason for choosing the name "Clara." However, some commentators have noted the relationship between the name "Clara" and the term "clairvoyance." Schelling's nickname for Pauline was his "oracle" and he often made reference to her clarity of thought. Thus perhaps Clara could represent Pauline. If so, his first daughter, Caroline, would have been named after his first wife and his second daughter, Clara, represented Pauline. "Pauline" would not have been possible as a name for their daughter because they had already called their first son "Paul." Another argument in support of Clara's representing Pauline is that the priest has at least four children (two older daughters and the younger children) and that the priest's wife has died. Similarly, if *Clara* was still being written as late as 1817, as Schelling's son claimed, then at this point Schelling too had four children (albeit by Pauline) and had a wife who had died. At Christmas Clara stands in as their mother, just as Pauline replaced Caroline. Shortly after Caroline's death Pauline also reported that Caroline had been like a second mother to her. She ended up being Schelling's second wife and the mother of his children and thus, as in the text, the relationship was inverted. Clara says that she feels as if she knew the mother, even though she never met her. Similarly, Pauline knew Caroline, but mostly only by correspondence.

Grau (1997) takes a different line of thought altogether. Grau argues that Schelling was more careful with names than to choose "Clara" just because it sounded similar to "Caroline." He suggests that the only historical Clara that comes into consideration is Clara of Assisi. She was born circa 1193-1194 and, under the influence of Francis of Assisi, left her parental home and lived away from society. She later became an abbot under the rules of the Benedictines and became a saint after her death. In Schelling's fragment, Clara also left her parental home and lived apart from society, Grau argues, and many of the discussions take place near a cloister.

These, then, are the major views that have been offered. If *Clara* was written immediately after Caroline's death, it appears most likely that Schelling chose the name "Clara" to reflect Caroline's earlier desire to be Schelling's Clärchen. Also, Schelling was convinced just after Caroline's death that she unconsciously knew that she was about to die. Even later he described Caroline as having a prophetic spirit without her knowing it. Hence the connection between "clairvoyance" and "Clara" could hold true for Caroline as well as for Pauline. If, however, some of *Clara* was written at a later stage, "Clara" could become representative of both women. On the whole, the relationship between the name "Clara" and "clairvoyance" seems to me to be the most compelling reason for the choice of name, especially given the large role that Schelling was to attach to clairvoyance in the sketch at the end of *Clara*. It is not clear that Clara represents just one of the women in Schelling's life; rather, she is inspired by them both.

As a philosophical work, though, *Clara* embodies and represents Schelling's views; no one character alone can be understood as Schelling, for it is in the interaction of the figures that the work—and Schelling's philosophy—come alive.

CLOSING REMARKS

This introduction has shown that even aside from the philosophical issues, *Clara* holds many mysteries for Schelling scholars. But *Clara* is also philosophically important. It is possible that a careful examination of the relationship between *Clara* and the "Stuttgart Seminars" may throw light on the development of Schelling's thought. I have already indicated that the "Stuttgart Seminars" are not as similar to *Clara* as many believe. Likewise, if Schelling was already composing *Clara* at the time of *Philosophie und Religion*, it may be useful to compare and contrast that work with *Clara* and *Of Human Freedom*. Brown (1996), for instance, has already argued that *Philosophie und Religion* and *Of Human Freedom* are not as alike as people have often assumed. If Schelling reworked *Clara* in this period, a comparison of the three texts may help track Schelling's progression of thought. Similarly, if *Clara* was a sketch for *The Ages of the World* or the start of its second or third book, a closer analysis of all these texts in relation to each other is required. Of course, this is a difficult task because there are many versions of *The Ages of the World* and we have only one of the remaining *Clara* versions—and only a fragment of both works. But it is also a fundamental task if Schelling scholars wish to understand better what *The Ages of the World* was or was not to contain. In addition, Schelling notably retains some of the thoughts in *Clara* many years later in his work. For example, in the *Urfassung der Philosophie der Offenbarung* (*Original Version of the Philosophy of Revelation*) that Schelling intended for publication and that Ehrhardt (1992) discovered only recently in the library at the University of Eichstaett, Schelling writes, "There are expressions that are the same in all languages. . . . One such expression is that one calls departed beings *spirits* and not souls. Here one thinks of the whole person, but [as] spiritualized or essentialized"

(596, my translation). In *Clara* the central focus is on "the whole person" surviving death, with the spiritual taking its uppermost turn as the person goes over into the next life. In *Clara*, Clara herself remarks that people describe what survives death as the "spirit" rather than as the "soul." The resemblances to *Clara* here are unmistakable, even though, by popular estimates, the two works are about thirty years apart. This serves as further evidence that the ideas in *Clara* were never completely forgotten by Schelling.

Grau (1997) wrote at the beginning of his essay on *Clara* that

> Indeed, Schelling is concerned not only with the spirit world in the metaphorical sense, but with the question of whether there is a life after death and in which form it could exist. Schelling's fragment thus comes across as a foreign body in his work which—and this impression becomes all the more apparent when you look at the Schelling bibliography—one would be better off ignoring. (my translation)

However, one should perhaps heed Schelling's own remarks in the introduction, where he notes that some people have a certain fear as soon as they come across the words "spirit world." That is, one should not ignore *Clara* because one is uncomfortable with the content; it is better to investigate the text and see whether it really is such a foreign body as it may first appear. It may turn out that up to now Schelling scholars have been closing their eyes just as it is time to wake up.

BIOGRAPHIES OF SCHELLING AND CAROLINE

I have not always cited my sources for each piece of biographical information, particularly where there is large-scale agreement. The following works were my main sources, lesser-used sources I have cited in the text, and a full set of references can be found at the end of the translation.

Gulyga, Arsenij. (1989). *Schelling: Leben und Werk.* Trans. E. Kirsten.

Kahn-Wallenstein, Carmen. (1959). *Schellings Frauen: Caroline und Pauline.*

Kirchhoff, Jochen. (1982). *Schelling.*

Kleßmann, Eckhart. (1975). *Caroline.*

LETTERS AND DOCUMENTS

Below I cite the works I used. All translations of letters and documents are my own. There is some overlap between the sources.

Braun, Otto. (1908). *Schelling als Persönlichkeit: Briefe, Reden, Aufsätze.*

Fuhrmans, Horst, ed. (1962, 1973, 1975). *F. W. J. Schelling: Briefe und Dokumente.*

Pareyson, Luigi, ed. (1977). *Schellingiana Raroria.*

Plitt, Gustav, ed. (1869). *Aus Schellings Leben: In Briefen.*

Tilliette, Xavier, ed. (1974, 1981). *Schelling im Spiegel seiner Zeitgenossen.*

Waitz, Georg, ed. (1913). *Caroline: Briefe aus der Frühromantik.*

Sandkühler (1998) lists a more complete set of sources for Schelling's correspondence. Many of Schelling's letters remain unpublished. Over one thousand are in the Schelling Archives in Berlin. For an important set of letters that have only recently been published and that suggest a romance in Schelling's later life, see Hahn (2000). See also Tilliette (1999) for a new biography of Schelling.

NOTES ABOUT THE TRANSLATION

Edition Translated

Clara remained as a fragment and was first published posthumously in Schelling's collected works under the title *On Nature's Connection to the Spirit World*. This title was given to the discussion by Schelling's son, K. F. A. Schelling. Shortly after the collected works had appeared, K. F. A. Schelling brought out *Clara* as a separate edition. It was only at this point that K. F. A. Schelling added "Clara" to the title. The work has been referred to as *Clara* ever since. Six single editions of *Clara* have appeared in German, each version differing with each new editor.

The *Clara* edition presented here follows the original version in the collected works (the separate edition brought out in 1862 omitted the introduction) and the numbers in square brackets in the translation generally refer to the page location in the *Sämmtliche Werke*. The only exception is the spring fragment and the sketch at the end. The spring fragment had not been published in the collected works and it was first printed in K. F. A. Schelling's two separate editions of *Clara* in 1862 and 1865. Thus the numbers in square brackets in the spring fragment refer to the pages in the first separate edition of *Clara*; these page numbers remained the same for K. F. A. Schelling's second edition of the text too. Although Schröter claimed in 1948 to be printing the spring fragment with *Clara* for the first time, the fragment had in fact already been published some seventy years before. There are slight differences between Schröter's version of the spring fragment and the one published earlier by Schelling's son and I have signaled these discrepancies within the text.

I have similarly indicated throughout where the various published single editions differ from each other. Most versions vary only in so far as they either include or exclude the introduction (only Kuhlenbeck [1913] keeps the introduction) or the spring fragment (only K. F. A. Schelling's first two editions and Schröter's 1948 edition published the spring fragment). However, Ehrenberg (1922) made the radical move of omitting everything that came after the discussion between Clara and the priest about how philosophy should best be presented to the public. Ehrenberg claimed that his version rounded off the text better and that the omitted discussions that followed were of inferior quality. No other editor has cut out these discussions. Schröter even added a sketch for the continuation of *Clara* in the epilogue to his edition and this sketch also has been included in the version published here. It has not appeared in any of the other single editions of *Clara*. Indeed, at present there is no single German edition of *Clara* that has all contested parts included within it. I hope that by including all pieces of text here, readers will be able to decide for themselves which sections they think do belong to *Clara*.

TRANSLATION DIFFICULTIES

I have included a German-English and English-German glossary to enable readers who know some German to identify how I have decided to translate some central terms.

As almost any English speaker interested in German philosophy will know, there is a perennial problem of how to distinguish in English translation the German noun *das Sein* from that of *das Seiende*. In English both terms would ordinarily be translated as "the being," although *das Sein* is a noun in the same way that in English *the laugh* is a noun, whereas *das Seiende* is the noun derived from the more active gerund, just as *the laughing* is also so derived. But whereas the distinction between these two types of words can be mirrored with the nominal derivatives of the verb *to laugh*, with the verb *to be* the differentiation disappears in translation. And the distinction is crucial in much of German philosophy.

In the past a relatively popular way of solving this translation problem has been to take over the German custom of capitalizing nouns, so that the noun *das Sein* is translated as "Being" (with an uppercase B) and *das Seiende* as "being" (with a lowercase b). However, this strategy places more work on the reader and means that typing or transcript errors are easily missed, thus resulting in yet further potential for the reader to be unwittingly misled. For this reason I have decided to translate *das Sein* with the rather clumsy "beingness" instead, in order to stress the fact that it is a noun. And to emphasize the activity inherent in *das Seiende* I have used the phrase *what actively is*.

Another difficulty that is particularly prevalent in *Clara* is Schelling's use of adjectives that have two meanings. Perhaps the most prevalent example is the adjective *dunkel* which can mean both "dark" and "obscure." Sometimes I have used both translations and have thus rendered *dunkel* as "dark and obscure"; at other times I have just selected one of the two alternatives. At some important points I have included the German word and added an explanatory endnote. However, this paragraph and the previous one should serve as reminders as to how often translation is really interpretation.

GENERAL INTRODUCTION   xxxix

Unlike English, German is a gendered language—each noun is either feminine, masculine, or gender neutral. As a consequence, there is less need for repetition of nouns in German because the gender of the word *it* makes it clear to which noun in the preceding sentence the author is referring. In English, however, *it* would be too ambiguous, so I have often replaced *it* by the relevant noun for clarity. I have not indicated these substitutions in the text.

FOOTNOTES AND ENDNOTES

Adding notes is always a two-edged sword. On the one hand, readers may appreciate having the information; on the other hand footnotes remove the power from readers to claim their own connections and discoveries about the text. Because most people wishing to use this text academically will probably be Schelling scholars, I have not made any attempt to connect *Clara* to other works of Schelling or, indeed, to other philosophical contexts. I will leave this path of discovery open. Instead, I have focused on the historical background to lend the text more color. My hope is that my endnotes will further support Schelling's aim in writing *Clara*—that is, that they will make the discussion feel more alive and immediate, as if it were something that really happened. I have taken the liberty of sometimes expanding the notes at length, if the appropriate sources were very old and are likely to be difficult to obtain by those living outside of Germany. Footnotes are always either by Schelling or his son and are in the original text; all endnotes, and any translations in those endnotes, are my own.

NUMBERING OF SECTIONS

In the original version of *Clara* the different sections are not numbered; they are simply separated from each other by a few blank lines. Following Schröter, I have added roman numerals at the beginning of each section in order to make it easier for commentators to refer to the relevant parts.

ACKNOWLEDGMENTS

Most of this translation was undertaken while I was employed at the Institut für Grenzgebiete der Psychologie und Psychohygiene e.V. [IGPP] in Freiburg, Germany. I would like to thank them for allowing me to pursue this work along side the project they employed me to do. My colleagues, Harriet Falkenhagen, Liane Hoffman, Michael Miener, Werner Plihal, and Christian Scheer, kindly read parts of the translation for me. I am indebted to Gabriela Böhm for reading the entire manuscript with a kind but critical eye. She and Daniele Baur had the task of deciphering my writing in order to compose the glossary. I will remember my days at the IGPP with gratitude and pleasure.

Additionally, I was delighted to be invited to Oglethorpe University, Atlanta, to give two seminars on *Clara*. Jason Wirth's German Idealism class gave the translation its first public test. Delpha Duggar deserves special mention for initiating the invitation and finding the funds for my flight, Veronica Holmes for offering me accommodation, and Penny Anderson for showing me around Atlanta.

I would like to thank Jason Wirth for his enthusiasm about this project. Walter Ehrhardt was good enough to read my introduction. He kindly made available to me some of his ongoing work on *Clara*. This enabled me to make considerable improvements both to my own introduction and to the editorial endnotes to the translation. Finally, I am grateful to the editorial staff at State University of New York Press for the many improvements they made to the entire manuscript.

Chronology

1763 2 September—Caroline Dorothea Albertine Michaelis is born in Göttingen. Father is Johann David Michaelis and mother is Luise Schröder.

1775 27 January—Friedrich Wilhelm Joseph Schelling is born in Leonberg. Father is Joseph Friedrich Schelling and mother is Gottliebin Maria Cleß.

1777 The Schelling family moves to Bebenhausen.

1781 Kant's *Critique of Pure Reason* is published.

1784 Caroline marries her first husband, the doctor Johann Franz Wilhelm Böhmer.

1785 28 April—Caroline gives birth to her first child, Auguste. Schelling attends the Latin School in Nürtingen.

1786 29 December—Pauline Gotter is born. Father is Johann Friedrich Wilhelm Gotter and mother is Luise Stieler. Schelling returns to Bebenhausen after he has outstripped his teachers' capacities at Nürtingen.

1787 23 April—Caroline gives birth to her second child, Therese.

1788 4 February—Johann Böhmer dies. Kant's *Critique of Practical Reason* is published. Goethe's *Egmont* is published.

1789 14 July—Storming of the Bastille in Paris. Beginning of the French Revolution.
17 December—Therese, Caroline's second child, dies.

1790 18 October—Schelling starts studying at the Tübinger Stift. Shares room with Hegel and Hölderlin. Kant's *Critique of Judgement* is published.

1793 30 March—Caroline arrested; she and Auguste are put in jail.
5 July—Caroline and Auguste are released from prison.
3 November—Out of wedlock, Caroline gives birth to her third child, Wilhelm Julius, whose father is Jean Baptiste Dubois-Crancé. The birth

	is entered under the names of Julie and Julius Krantz; godfather is listed as Friedrich Schlegel.
1794	Schelling publishes *Über die Möglichkeit einer Form der Philosophie*. Fichte publishes *Grundlage der gesamten Wissenschaftslehre*.
1795	30 April—Wilhelm Julius, Caroline's third child, dies. Schelling publishes *Vom Ich als Prinzip der Philosophie*. Schelling graduates from the Tübinger Stift. November. Schelling is employed as a private tutor. Goethe publishes *Unterhaltungen deutscher Ausgewanderten*.
1796	1 July—Caroline marries August Wilhelm Schlegel.
1797	Schelling is called to an unpaid chair at Jena.
1800	12 July—Auguste, Caroline's first child, dies in Bad Bocklet, aged fifteen.
1802	Schelling publishes four poems—*Die letzten Worte des Pfarrers, Lied, Pflanze und Tier*, and *Los der Erde*—in *Musenalmanach für das Jahr 1802*, under the pseudonym of Bonaventura. Schelling publishes the discussion *Bruno: Or, on the Natural and the Divine Principle of Things*. Schelling publishes the dialogue "Über das absolute Identitäts-System und sein Verhältnis zu dem neuesten (Reinholdischen) Dualismus. Ein Gespräch zwischen dem Verfasser und einem Freund" in the *Kritisches Journal*. Summer—Anonymous article (by Berg) published by Schütz in the *Allgemeine Literaturzeitung* accusing Schelling of murding Auguste. October—Wilhelm Schlegel publishes a pamphlet in defense of Schelling, "An das Publikum. Rüge einer in der Jenaischen ALZ begangenen Ehrenschädigung." Schütz replies in his article "Secies facti nebst Aktenstücken zum Beweisen, daß Hr. Rath AW Schlegel . . ." but he does not retract the accusation that Schelling was ultimately responsible for Auguste's death.
1803	17 May—Caroline and Wilhelm Schlegel get divorced. 26 June—Caroline and Schelling marry. Schelling called to a paid chair at Würzburg.
1804	Schelling publishes *Philosophy and Religion*. Renewed accusations that Schelling was responsible for Auguste's death appear in the press. Goethe publishes *Die natürliche Tochter*.
1805	Autumn—Würzburg falls to Austria.
1806	18 April—Schelling leaves Würzburg and goes to Munich.
1807	Schelling publishes his experiments on the dowser Campetti. Windischmann publishes his discussions *Von der Selbstvernichtung der Zeit und der*

CHRONOLOGY   xliii

Hoffnung zur Wiedergeburt [On the Self-Destruction of Time and the Hope of Rebirth].
Summer—Hegel sends Schelling a copy of his *Phänomenologie des Geistes* so that Schelling could write a review of it.
12 October—Schelling gives speech ("*Über das Verhältnis der bildenden Künste zu der Natur*") for the king's name day at the Bavarian Academy of Sciences.

1808   Schelling made General Secretary of the Bavarian Academy of Arts in Munich. Schubert publishes *Ansichten von der Nachtseite der Wissenschaft* [Views from the Night-Side of Science]. Jung-Stilling publishes *Theorie der Geister-Kunde* [Theory of Spirit-Knowledge].

1809   May—Schelling publishes *Of Human Freedom*.
7 September—Caroline dies in Maulbronn, aged 46.
Goethe's *Die Wahlverwandschaften* is published.

1810   Schelling gives the Stuttgart Seminars (published posthumously).

1812   28 May—Schelling meets Pauline Gotter at Lichtenfels to see if she would be a suitable marriage partner.
11 June—Pauline and Schelling marry.

1813   17 December—Pauline gives birth to Paul.

1815   2 August—Pauline gives birth to Friedrich.
12 October—Schelling gives speech "*Die Gottheiten von Samothrake*."

1817   25 March—Pauline gives birth to Caroline.

1818   3 July—Pauline gives birth to Clara.

1821   20 July—Pauline gives birth to Julia.

1824   19 April—Pauline gives birth to Hermann.

1831   14 November—Hegel dies in Berlin.

1840   Schelling called to the chair in Berlin to replace Hegel.

1841   15 November—Schelling's first lecture in Berlin.

1846   Schelling finishes lecturing in Berlin.

1854   20 August—Schelling dies in Bad Ragaz (Switzerland), aged 79.
13 December—Pauline dies in Gotha, aged 67.

Clara

or, On Nature's Connection to the Spirit World

F. W. J. SCHELLING

Introduction

[3] Ever since the peaceful harmony broke up in which the sciences lived not so long ago, philosophy can be characterized as an intense striving toward the spiritual that decidedly lacks a corresponding capacity to rise to it.[i]

Through its name the old metaphysics declared itself to be a science that followed in accordance with, and that to some extent also followed from, our knowledge of nature and improved and progressed from that; thus in a certain competent and sound way that is of service only to those who have a desire for knowledge, metaphysics took the knowledge that it boasted in addition physics. Modern philosophy did away with its immediate reference to nature, or didn't think to keep it, and proudly scorned any connection to physics. Continuing with its claims to a higher world, it was no longer metaphysics but hyperphysics. Only now did its complete incapacity for its proposed aim emerge. Because it wanted to spiritualize itself completely, it first of all threw away [4] the material that was absolutely necessary to the process and right from the very beginning it kept only what was spiritual. But what is to become of the spiritual if it is spiritualized again? Or if we want everything spiritual to be within nature already, what do we have left for the spirit world?

These remarks will serve to make comprehensible the strange phenomenon that just when philosophy wanted to take its highest approach to the spiritual, it sank to the very bottom and became more and more inadequate and incapable in relation to all higher objects. After a period of seeing this happen, it finally came to be felt intensely that there was nothing else left for philosophy to do than to testify against itself—not only to recognize its spiritual impotency, but also to demonstrate the obviousness of such. Meanwhile, this conclusion was also used to drive the spiritualization yet another degree further away. It was not enough, one said, to have given up the connection to what is objective or to insensible nature, if so

---

i. Note by K. F. A. Schelling: This introduction, it appears, was originally intended not for a discussion but for a treatise. Nevertheless, it belongs to the following discussion insofar as it was to have essentially the same content, the treatise having the title "Presentation of the transition from a philosophy of nature to a philosophy of the spirit world"; moreover, the introduction was found bound up with the discussion. A small part of an outline for this treatise remains in the handwritten literary estate.

coarse a concept as that of knowledge were still tolerated within the subjective. Knowledge itself was still too solid; spiritualization would be perfect only when, instead, a tender, fleeting spoor of a feeling or hunch alone remains; that is, when the subjective is subjectified again. Since then one party occupied itself with offering a surrogate of the spirit (of knowledge) rather than the true spirit; the surrogate supposedly being somehow more spiritual than the spirit itself. And so, whereas previously a virtue was made of necessity, a virtue was now made of ignorance.

In this state of affairs there was indeed no other means of restoring philosophy than by calling it back to earth—albeit not from heaven, which it had renounced, but from that empty space in which it was suspended between heaven and earth. This happened through the philosophy of nature. Nevertheless, it was only to be expected from the general order and run of things that the spiritualizers of this time would clamor that this beginning was bringing philosophy down, denying everything spiritual, even denying what was holy and divine.

[5] Yet right from the start nature was explained only as one side of the universe, with the spirit world opposed to it. Thus, even the philosophy of nature was given always as only one side of the larger picture, and the central role of philosophical science resided in scientifically explaining the contradictions and connections between nature and the spirit world. Now that we have satisfactorily undertaken this exercise in our first steps in philosophy, it can be predicted that to those philosophers this beginning appears to be one that is superficial, fanciful even, and in any case unnatural. For doesn't it so happen that as soon as their own concepts and theories go beyond nature, these too take on a truly unnatural character and thereby prove themselves ineffectual for daily life? Yes, here those philosophers will become friends with those with whom they previously professed to be in conflict but with whom they are really more united than they themselves believe; I mean those who can't hear the words *spirit world* without getting caught up in their own particular fear of "spirit." This sickness in its strongest form may rise to fear and to granting only that man's own innermost being is spirit, but in its weakest form limits itself to a concern with cutting oneself off from the spirit world completely and ensuring there is no belief in any spirit other than one's own and those of one's contemporaries.

Now the adherents of both philosophies would have the completely wrong idea of our undertaking if they thought that here the spirit world is to be brought immediately to light [Erkenntnis] in some way or even brought only to articulation, for our express intention is only scientifically to show the natural field's transition to the field of the spiritual world. Thus, insofar as nature is our starting point, it would be best for them to see this treatise as a purely physicalistic one and to grasp the idea that just as in the physical [world] it has been possible to bind earth to heaven through the law of gravity, and just as we may flatter ourselves [6] for having placed the golden chain of universally-extending light in friendly concourse with the distant stars that barely come to view even when we equip our eyes with the strongest means, so too within the spiritual [world] a tie may be found going out from nature through which our as yet merely earthly sciences could continually rise up toward heaven, for heaven does indeed appear to be their true fatherland.

For now it is up to them to deny such an upward growth of nature into the spiritual world, and they will deny it. However, unless they deny the existence of a spirit world altogether—a debate which is not our concern here—they admit that nature is subordinate to the spirit world. Thus, in relation to the higher the subordinate has at some point its limit; somewhere it has a definite end. Now, how can they believe that the subordinate can find its goal and be closed, unless the last thing that it brings forth from itself is already something that goes beyond it and that belongs to it only with the subordinate part of its essence, just as man is in relation to the earth? And in being the rung to it, mustn't the lower thereby be in a *natural* relation to the higher?

Thus, before they can raise their usual complaints against this undertaking, they will first have to prove that there is such a chasm between nature and the purely spiritual world as they assume, or at least they will have to knock down our proofs that there is a natural connection between them. Only with this qualification do we consider it possible to do justice to the proposed exercise. We ourselves recognize that any knowledge that doesn't develop purely from what is present and real is one that is superficial and that has to lead to fanciful imagination and error. Just because of that we declare that however far we may care to drive the edifice of our thoughts in what follows, we will still only have achieved something if the temple whose last spire disappears into an inaccessible light is, at its very deepest foundation, wholly supported by nature.

On the other hand, we will thus certainly dare to take on whatever [7] he who knows of a sound basis permits us to do, and we will be able to explain higher things with more certainty than has been possible until now. A person earns, so to speak, the right to the most spiritual objects only when he has already taken care to understand their opposite. In his undertakings, even scientific ones, man errs not through what he undertakes to do, but in the way he does it; namely by not taking his knowledge step by step; meanwhile nothing is in fact denied, not even within science, to him who meets that condition. A tree that draws strength, life, and substance into itself from the earth may hope to drive its topmost branches hanging with blossom right up to heaven. However, the thoughts of those who think from the beginning that they can separate themselves from nature, even when they are truly spiritually and mentally gifted, are only like those delicate threads that float in the air in late summer and that are as incapable of touching heaven as they are of being pulled to the ground by their own weight.

Fully conscious of the scientific means required by the nature of our procedure, we won't bring anything into play that isn't essential or that could otherwise lead us astray.

In this discourse one will rarely find flights of imagination, particularly ones sought within the external, or find those certain lighthearted talks about the immortality of the soul that both writers and public alike seem so very much to enjoy. We don't want to excite people's opinions or foster a fanciful imagination, for these always arise mainly out of the shortcomings or inadequacies of science. If science remains silent about the things man finds to be the most essential of all, then people must indeed come to their own aid. How far ahead they are of the educated in their certitude of thought! Our moralistic and other proofs for the immortality of the soul would not suffice for the people. Common sense comprehends that the true basis that persuades it [that sense] of some kind of existence must at the same time necessarily give us knowledge of how that existence is constituted, and common sense will consider any basis for which this is not [8] the case to be invented and artificial rather than one that is true and natural. But even now it still holds, as it has for ages, that the scholars have thrown away the keys to knowledge and although they themselves don't go therein, they refuse to let in those who wish to enter. Even the refuge in the truths of revelation—which was the last refuge that remained to the people—is taken from them, with the teachers of these truths interpreting them either literally or only in a general, moralistic sense. The learned know in what kind of light they appear when a real sense is attached to these truths and the physical relationship is given. The chasm between revelation and science comes about just because the former contains all truths within it, truths pursued from the very beginning and to a degree of individual certainty that our philosophy, forever drifting about in generalities, could not yet achieve.

Thus, one shouldn't suspect those seeking certainty of knowledge, even in the most spiritual objects, of fanciful imagination or of trying to lead people to so imagine; rather, one should suspect those who work against that certainty, even if they should do so with the pretext of having a sense that supersedes science itself. When superstition completely overlooks the natural connection of things, nonbelief results; and it results from the suffocation of the divine stirring in its innermost being, the suffocation itself resulting from nonbelief's not being able to set natural mass into motion, from its being unable to transform that mass into a living, progressive surge up to the spiritual. Belief, which acts as the opposite of science, is in exactly the same situation. But it is impossible for a belief that follows from an initial nonbelief and that shares the same starting point as nonbelief to be a true one.

But, even looking at it purely from a formal standpoint, the real dreamers are without doubt those who regard the world of science as a great empty space wherein each person in his own peculiar way can record whatever takes his fancy. They are those who have [9] no idea of how to go back to the basics and construct anything systematically. They are those who, when they ask themselves what they know with certainty from their philosophical endeavors, have to admit, if they are at all honest with themselves, that they do not even know so much as is required, for example, for taking notes from a book in some language or other, whereby one must know whether one should read from left to right or, as in Hebrew, from right to left.

Insofar as his concern is purely to achieve an effect, an author can hardly fail to achieve his aim with a subject that bears a manifold and intimate relationship to the deepest feelings of human kind, if he knows how to introduce these feelings in an unobtrusive and pleasant way. However, he who tries to produce these feelings by using precise-scientific insight must wish to silence them from the beginning. The inclination will become naught, even if a justifiable longing is accorded to it; with his scientific earnestness increasing with the magnitude of the subject, he will ask only about whatever can be ascertained scientifically and will deny himself for the sake of the invaluable gain of an everlasting truth. The deepest feeling is fully confirmed only within a science that does not combine with that feeling; a combination of the two is scorned by both. He only hopes that he will never find himself in contradiction with faith, hope, and love; and he never will have a low opinion of anything that is inspired by them just because he can't scientifically justify it, if, like the poet, we may suppose that in those bright realms there is a word for every beautiful and pleasant feeling. But, although faith, hope, and love are that innermost, sacred essence that gives all works of science and art their last transfiguration, in their more intimate nature they have to appear as one or the other to be a visible principle.

In taking responsibility for conveying our thoughts in a more accessible form, too, we will favor the stricter form and we will, where possible, give an example in this treatise of a method that differs from those heretofore in so far as it is quite [10] inseparable from its content, with the method being given through the content, as the content is through the method. Unavoidably, more than a few of its formulae have been most shamefully misused (whose innermost being no one has yet completely penetrated), by treating what is most living mainly with reason. On the other hand, we have noticed that in cases of real investigation where, perhaps without knowing it, the formulae have been conceded to have a certain influence, the method proves itself to be more beneficial than the usual one; proving that in various areas the current standing of science is beginning to call for this method. Whoever wants to change this method mustn't attack the spiritless use of it, nor in any way the method itself; he must attack the substance.[1]

I

[11] THE PRIEST NARRATES

On All Souls' Day the doctor and I rode into town in order to pick up Clara in the evening, Clara having traveled in a few days earlier in the company of my two daughters.[1] As we came to an opening that framed the pretty town, lying midway or so up the mountain within the backdrop of the broad plain, we saw a crowd of people thronging toward a gentle incline that lay to one side. We guessed immediately where this train of people was headed and we joined them so that for once we, too, could watch the moving festival dedicated to the dead that is celebrated this day in Catholic towns. We found the whole area full of people already. It was peculiar to see life on the graves, forebodingly illuminated by the dully shining autumn sun. As we left the trodden path, we soon saw pretty groups gathered around individual graves: here girls in their bloom, holding hands with their younger brothers and sisters, crowned their mother's grave; there at the grave of her children lost so young a mother stood in silence with no need for consecrated water to represent her tears, for tears sanctified by sweet melancholy flowed gently down to freshen the mounds. Here and there men stood seriously and contemplatively in front of individual graves that held an early departed friend or perhaps a girlfriend they would never forget. Here, all of life's severed relationships were revived for the spectator who was familiar with the people [12] and the circumstances; brothers came again to brothers and children to parents; at this moment all were one family again. Only the loved one who had had her beloved snatched away by death could not appear in this crowd; she had perhaps chosen the early hours in which to cover the beloved place with her tears, all alone with the morning dew. The beautiful monument of a youth who died here as a stranger was decorated with flowers in such a delicate and thoughtful way that it must have been done by loving hands. How moving this custom is, my companion said, and how meaningful it is that the graves should be decorated with species that are late flowering: isn't it fitting that these autumn flowers should be consecrated to the dead, who hand us cheerful flowers from their dark chambers in spring as the eternal witness to the continuation of life and to the eternal resurrection.

In the middle of the square stood a small chapel incapable of holding the crowd. Soon after our arrival it had filled up so much that a long queue formed from the doors way across the graves. We sat to one side on an old and mossy gravestone whose inscription had long become illegible and we listened to the festive office, whose course we could follow only from the reactions of those who stood outside. We sat sunk in silent melancholy. How many of those who were now walking on the graves would be lying beneath them in the following year?

Where might our friend be tarrying? A few times we thought that we had seen her from afar, but without really being able to identify her or to get any closer to her in the crowd. We remembered that we still had a long way to go. She had told us that, in any case, we would find her at the time of departure at the other end of town, in a Benedictine cloister on a hill. We saw that it was time and we left in silence.

In the town everything was empty and deserted; we only stayed long enough to get some refreshments and then we climbed up to the [13] beautiful cloister. On arrival we were shown into the library, where a young, well-educated clergyman awaited us who seemed to have the duty of receiving guests and making conversation with them. We soon learned from him that the recently deceased prince had sent him on various journeys and that he had now become both the supervisor of this collection of books and the teacher of the philosophical sciences in the cloister. He showed us several rarities that were entrusted to his care. However, we were more drawn to the magnificent view from the windows, which looked out onto the distant plain and up to the hill where we had been earlier, than to these dead treasures. The plain was covered with towns and villages and the powerful river wound through it, becoming visible in places as if it were only a thin, silver ribbon [*Band*].[2]

He had already told us beforehand that we would have to wait here for Clara, who still had to speak to the prior of the cloister about certain affairs; several of the cloister's goods were locked up with those of her family, and some of her forebears' goods, too, were to be found in the care of his most excellent benefactor. Some of the portraits that were hanging in the hall, he explained, were of those very forebears; even the brother of one of them was portrayed in his monastic habit. We learned that he had sincerely dedicated himself to his profession and that he had died and been buried here. Had we doubted the clergyman in the slightest, the striking resemblance between the picture and our friend would have been enough to have persuaded us of the truth of what he was saying. We couldn't express enough amazement about this resemblance coming back two centuries later, and the clergyman opined that such a sight could well provoke belief in the transmigration of souls.

What is even more peculiar, I said, is that perhaps just as great a resemblance prevails between the fates of these two distant relatives as between their external appearances, and from the latter one would take them to be at least brother and sister. Who knows what led this earlier brother (for such I must call him) to these solitary walls and drove him to see out his days in seclusion. [14] Perhaps they were circumstances similar to those that make our friend prefer the peace of our quiet valley so much to life in the world or even in a larger town. Both of us have often requested that she move, for we believe that the solitude that continually keeps all her memories alive will undermine her health in the long run.

So, the clergyman said, she still lives in that secluded house where I visited her six years ago?

The very same one, I answered. Years ago a stranger had bought the land for it and built it; while fleeing six years ago she found it lying empty, bought it at a relatively low price, with the garden and vineyards that belonged to it, and she is living there again, for she has been expelled once more from the paternal estates.

At that time, the clergyman said, she had no relationship with our cloister; I had to steal the visit in secret, driven by a curiosity blended with silent respect. Certainly they were painful circumstances in which she found herself; and the late prelate of our cloister, who had always had a lot of influence on the family, was particularly against the marriage with a Protestant, as was, indeed, the whole of the Catholic nobility in the neighborhood—for, as the last heiress, through her all the beautiful goods passed on to the other side. Today is the very first visit that she has paid to our cloister, which, if I remember correctly, she had entered only a few times as a child with her parents. The sole ownership of such considerable goods, which she has now disavowed, changed things perhaps; besides, the present director is more open-minded and he has a better judgment of these times, in which everyone should be thinking about mutual deliverance rather than about feeding secret disputes.

The doctor, who until now had been spending his time enjoying the various pictures, broke in here with the words: It seems to me that the difference between our times and the previous ones becomes no more apparent [15] than in such a collection of portraits. These princes from the Thirty Years' War and earlier—how solid their heads are, how cultivated and proud they are from every angle.[3] Look at the foreheads and eyes that these soldiers have, as do those distinguished for their actions, and whom we now see here side by side! I would like to know whether any single one of the last male offspring of these families carries such an expression of great spiritual feeling and strength of character in himself as this head does, and whether the dying out of the lineage hasn't simply brought the forbears' higher traits into the female form instead?

At that very moment Clara entered the room in the highest of spirits, and only now did the resemblance become so frighteningly apparent that we all had to stop ourselves from betraying what we were feeling. For I don't know why each of us avoided sharing this observation with her or, alternatively, why we let it only be guessed. The direction of her eyes drew me toward the open window, and as she caught sight of the blue and remote hills, her eyes filled with tears and she said: Behind those hills yonder, which will become bluer and bluer and over which the sun is now about to sink, there lies buried everything I have. Oh Albert, Albert, we had to leave the quiet sanctuary that united us on this side, only to be separated for so long—oh, who knows how long. Hardly have I lost you when I am chased away yet again, and I am torn away even from that small area of ground that covers you, which was the very last thing I had of you. Robbers desecrate the graves of my fathers; yet you slumber with them. Today even the poorest people go to visit their loved ones' graves; I alone could not go to adorn yours. Yet my tears flow here peacefully and purely; whatever part of the earth receives them, they penetrate their way to you by a magical force and refresh you in your grave.

I was alarmed by such a quick and unexpected passion and I hoped to cut it short by trying to link the discussion to general things. I grant you, I said, this commemoration of the dead has had a strong effect on me. It has become [16] so clear to me again how the life that we now live is a completely one-sided one and that it will become complete only if what is more highly spiritual could combine with it and if those, whom we call deceased, were not to stop living with us, but were simply to make up, as it were, another part of the whole family. The ancient Egyptian practices have something terrible about them, but they are based on a thought that is in itself true and correct.[4] We should support all festivals and customs in which we are reminded of a connection with the world beyond.

Forgive me, broke in the clergyman, who had drawn closer in the meantime and who had heard the last words, but I feel I have to express another opinion here. Now, today's commemoration, for example, certainly has something moving about it; however, if its purpose is to support the thought that we can be connected to the inhabitants of that other world, then I would hold this commemoration to be one that is almost detrimental and I would submit that it be abolished in your church, as so many others have been. Since no one responded, he continued: We who are living are allocated to this world only once; here we should do as much good as we can, we should show our every love and trust to those to whom we are close and we should do so for as long as we remain with them on their path. And we would certainly fulfill this duty to each other far more closely and conscientiously if we were continually to remind ourselves of their mortality—that at their death any connection we have to them will be removed and that then neither the passion of our love can reach them nor that of our hate, our low disposition.

Perhaps, Clara replied, the lower cannot act on the higher, but it is more certain that the higher can act within the lower, and thus the thought of some community would not be so inconsistent.

If, that is, the clergyman continued, both of them are within one and the same world, as spirit and body belong to one world in our present life. However, the deceased are quite dead in respect of this sensible world and they can't possibly bring forth an effect in a region for which their tools are as limited as their receptivity.

[17] Your speech, I said to him, reminds me of the explanation which our philosophizing theologians give today of the wonder of God's extraordinary effect on the sensible world, without thinking how much of this world is itself completely nonsensible.

Nevertheless, he replied, we must honor these old divisions. A reasonable person could see only with regret how these divisions are shifting, that everything is now flowing into everything else without any differentiation at all, and that soon we will not be completely at home in either one world or the other.

But you yourself grant, Clara said, that at least in us something else lives, something that is other than a mere material essence: the spirit. You will therefore also have to admit that through this latter we really do have a link to that world and that, even if we accept that the material is cut off from the spiritual, there is no proof against a possible connection between what is spiritual in us and the powers of another world.

Granted, he answered, if our spirit really could ever rise up to pure spirituality. That is, if, through its link to matter, the spirit were not completely separated from the purity of the world to which it is supposed to rise only after this tie has been broken.

With such a complete separation, I replied, you must also reject any concept of that higher world.

Indeed, it is so, he answered: any concept of it that reason or understanding may want to form. We have within us a single point that is open and through which heaven shines in. This is our heart or, to be more precise, our conscience. In the latter we find one law and one purpose, a purpose that cannot be from this world, for more often than not it is in conflict with it. Thus, for us it serves as a pledge from a higher world and it raises him who has learned to follow it to the comforting thought of immortality.

And to nothing more? Clara responded. The word "immortality" [18] seems to me to be far too weak for the impression I have. What do cold words and merely negative concepts have to do with ardent [heiße] longing?[5] Are we satisfied in this life with a purely bleak existence? Does nature make us put up with such generalities?

Belief is simple, he answered, as is the duty from which it comes.

You make out that you are basing the greatest or highest certainty within the heart and yet you don't give the heart any credit at all. We cannot watch an old friend go away, whose duty calls him far away from us, without our thoughts following him to those remote places, without our vividly imagining his location and surroundings, without our wanting to know whether he has kept his old habits or whether he has changed them.

A separation in this life is one thing, he said, and the transition into a world with nothing in common with this world is another.

For me it seems otherwise, I said. The opposite is itself precisely what is nearest. Deserts, mountains, distant lands, and seas can separate us from a friend in this life; the distance between this life and the other is no greater than that between night and day or vice versa. A heartfelt thought, together with our complete withdrawal from anything external, transfers us into that other world, and perhaps this other world becomes all the more hidden from us, the nearer to us it is.

I do not deny that, he answered. The spiritual world may merge with us, but our lives do not merge with it. Our view always remains restricted to our inner being and it cannot follow the destiny of departed friends, which I regard anyhow as a kind of selfish love.

How so? asked Clara.

Even in this life we so easily imagine that our friends and companions through life are *ours*, when really they are only God's; they are free beings, subject only to the One. We enjoy them only as a gift; death reminds us of this even if nothing else does, although it would seem wise always to remember even in life that there isn't anything we can call ours in the true sense of the word, that the vows of poverty, [19] deprivation, and in particular obedience are vows taken in relation to a higher and hidden will and are vows that each person should take upon himself. Although we would become all the more cautious about making the goods that we use completely our own—particularly, however, those finest goods of all, which we call love and friendship—if we remembered that the essence of the soul—which we may indeed draw unto us with the full force of our spirit and our heart, and yes, if it were possible, which we would fuse with our existence—is only in God's hand and that it is to God's hand that we must sooner or later entrust it. A moment nevertheless comes when the soul no longer belongs to us, but belongs once more to the whole, when it returns home into its original freedom and perhaps, in accordance with God's will, begins a new course that will never meet our own again and that serves to fulfill a quite different purpose from what it fulfilled here in working to develop our inner being and ennobling our essence.

So, Clara said, you don't believe that in friendship and love there is something that is by its very nature eternal, a tie that God has joined that neither death nor God himself could break. Thousands of relationships may break apart in this life, perhaps they only ever affected our inner being in a hostile or at least disturbing way, but the tie of a truly divine love is as unbreakable as the essence of the soul in which it is founded and is as eternal as a word from God. If children had been given to me and then they were all taken away, I could never consider it as chance or a temporary fortune to have been the mother of these souls; I would feel—yes, I would know—that they belong to me eternally and I to them and that no power on Earth or in heaven could take them from me or me from them.

Certainly, he answered, that is the true maternal feeling—yet, even here, in itself the natural relationship doesn't produce that eternal feeling, rather it is the feeling that makes the relationship eternal; for how else could there be so many unnatural mothers? This shows us that only our attitude is truly eternal. And if we can consider those natural relationships with some devotion [20], those relationships that arise despite ourselves, that an invisible hand joins, that have for themselves a divine confirmation—

Don't you believe, Clara interrupted, that other higher relationships, such as love and friendship, are also of a divine nature; that a quiet, unconscious, but thereby all the more compelling, necessity draws one soul to another?

I do not deny, he said, the workings of such a natural power, although I don't quite understand it. But once man has come into this conflict and contradiction with nature—and this I understand just as little, too—but once a deep depravity has taken root in man's nature such that he no longer has the capacity to draw purely from one or the other source of life and it is almost as dangerous to direct man toward freedom as it is to direct him toward necessity—as regards this I confess that after such an aberration I am highly doubtful about any relationship in which freedom plays even only a part and I do not venture lightly into this labyrinth. I let justice be done to the warmth of each beautiful heart, only let us take care not to shape the inspiration of feelings and the inventions of longing into general truths; for then there will no longer be any divisions. The grim and unruly mind will have the same right as the bright and ordered one, and we know what monsters have arisen from this drive to realize creatures from uncontrolled longing or from wild imagination.

The doctor, for whom this discussion hadn't seemed to be right for some time, spoke up here and said: You are right, only the most ordered minds should occupy themselves with the question of a life hereafter, only bright and joyful minds should approach these regions of eternal joy and peace. No one should devote themselves to this investigation until they have gained a firm and solid ground here, within nature, on which they can base their thoughts. Only those who understand our current life should speak about death and a hereafter. Any skimming over of our current condition, any knowledge that hasn't developed purely from what is present and real and that tries to anticipate something [21] to which the spirit wouldn't naturally have led is reprehensible and leads to fanciful imagination and error.

In this way, said the clergyman, would you reject all knowledge about things in the hereafter, as I do; for who, indeed, could say that they have understood life?

I do not know, the doctor replied, whether anyone can say that; but I do know that I don't consider it to be absolutely impossible. We simply mustn't seek it too high up, we mustn't cut the root off right at the beginning, which draws strength, life, and substance into itself from nature's soil and which can then, indeed, push its blooms right up to the heavens. And we must especially give up the thought of deriving life from something different and higher, as if we were simply wanting to grasp that. Not "top down" but "bottom up" is my motto. And, I believe, this motto is also quite appropriate to the humility that is so fitting for us in many respects. However, he added, I see that the sun is already setting behind the hills and I am concerned about our friend and the autumn evening air; so let us set off.

Clara quickly bade farewell with a glance toward the distant hills, and once my daughters had been picked up from town we rode back down again toward the mountain entrance and our valley. We sat together in silence and Clara was quiet and pensive. Finally, the doctor brought up a discussion about monastic life: Why do people usually think that monastic life is so pleasant and beautiful? Is it because everyone likes to think that behind the monk's habit there lies the ideal of a clear and peaceful person who has found his own equilibrium; an ideal that everyone wants to realize, but which they nevertheless don't know how to? For certainly only the mob can be influenced by external motivations, the life of luxury, the carefreeness of this state, and similar such things.

Only the beautiful location of the cloisters could win me over, Theresa said, the hills on which they are so often built, the fertile valleys that surround them.

[22] Isn't it the case, I said, that each of us has the vague feeling that bliss lies in not possessing anything, for possessions cause worry and responsibility. And because poverty and privation are hard and painful things, monastic life has to appear as a true ideal, for there everyone lives a happy and leisurely life without possessing anything.

It seems to me, Clara said, that anything that is unchanging inspires us with a feeling of deep respect, just as its opposite decreases our esteem. People whom I see living normal lives always appear to me to be essentially fluctuating and uncertain. Who knows whether the person, whom I now see acting with greatness [groß] and truth, will not subsequently be bowed down by the force of circumstances and will later act timidly [kleinmütig] and against his heart.[6] Who knows whether the person who today appears clear, free, and pure will not sooner or later become eclipsed, shackled, and torn apart by a violent passion. The person who makes a resolution about his whole life and who makes it in such a way that he calls God and the world as his witness, who makes this resolution under conditions which stamp it with the seal of indissolubility, and if I understand him as acting levelheadedly and through his own free will, it is *this* person who will always waken my respect. Why else do we say that prior to death no one is blessed apart from him, we might say, who dies while living—and what else is this solemn vow of deprivation and renunciation of worldly things other than a death in the living body?

It surprises me, I said, that none of us has cited the beneficent effect that a carefree seclusion could have on the arts and sciences.

Could, answered the doctor, but that it hasn't had for some time now; and then we would only have learned works and the hard work of those who put together collections to cite as proof thereof.

Nevertheless, I answered, the arts and learning would suffer more than a little if all these rich cloisters with their magnificent buildings, their considerable collections of books, their churches [23] with their many altar pieces, their murals, and their artistic wood carvings were to disappear.

Yes, said Theresa, and the whole area would become dreary. Indeed, I don't know what sight is more beautiful than a magnificent building with towers and domes rising up in the middle of nature's riches, surrounded by rippling cornfields with water, woods, and vineyards in the distance, where everywhere everything is alive with the hustle and bustle of people. The most beautiful town does not have this effect on me; it represses nature such that only at some distance from the city can nature come to be found once more. But the simplicity of mixing the unbounded richness of a country district with what is magnificent and great, this alone is what is true and fitting.

But then, I said, my Theresa would have to include castles and the nobility's beautiful country seats, too.

Oh no, she answered, above all I love constancy, where I see things keeping or staying together. Even in our time goods pass from one hand to another, one family dies out, nobility moves into the city, and if they ever move out of the city it is only in order to offend the peace and quiet of these beautiful valleys with their contrasting way of life and their loud entertainment.

You are right, my child, I responded, but don't forget that your point of view on the subject can't be the one that is generally held, at least not in the wild times we are facing now. Of the significance that these institutions once held, they have perhaps kept only the picturesque. However, one will find it easier and more agreeable to close down the institutions altogether than to restore them in accordance with their original aim in a way that would be appropriate for our times. When I see such a quiet cloister down below in the valley, or go past one on a hill from which it looks down, I have often thought to myself: if one day the time should come for all these monuments of a bygone time, please let at least one of our princes think to preserve one or two of these sanctuaries, to keep the buildings and their goods together, and to endow them to the arts and sciences. [24] However, only he who really lives within the spirit—the true academic and artist— is truly spiritual. Merely exercising piety as a way of life, without combining it with lively and active scientific research, leads to emptiness and eventually even to that mechanicalness devoid of heart and soul that would itself have belittled monastic life even in times such as ours. In those centuries when knowledge did not spread far, when monks were the only depositories of science and knowledge, they were also the true clergymen, the truly spiritual; since then the rest of the world has outstripped them so powerfully that they have increasingly ceased to be spiritual any more. The sciences have the same end as religion; their best times were and are those in which they are in accord with it. However, if there are countries in which the cloisters were reordered into schools when the change in faith came about, then that is not what I meant.

So what do you mean? the doctor asked.

What I meant was this: it is here on this hill that the next great German poem should be composed, it is here in this valley that a Platonic academy should gather, like that in Cosentina. Men from all of the arts and sciences should live a truly spiritual life here, in harmony and free from worry: they shouldn't be locked up in towns, in the constrictive conditions of society and far from nature. For the German spirit loves solitude as it loves freedom; anything conventional oppresses it. Unlike the tame scholar or poet who puts on whatever appearance so-called society desires and takes its praise and applause, the fodder of vanity, from society's hands and lips as he also takes the fodder of his physical needs, the German spirit loves to roam through woods, hills, and valleys, suckled only by nature's breast. The German spirit is not like a regular river that is dammed in and flows through only prescribed banks and countries; it is like the moistness in the earth whose secret pathways no one explores. This moistness nevertheless penetrates and stimulates everything wherever it goes; it gushes forth clear and free, unconcerned whether someone happens along this path and refreshes himself therein, but strengthens and refreshes him who does not shun the [25] solitary mountain tracks, the cliffs, and the remote valleys. It is a shame that after fully developing all of this in my head, I often have to tell myself that it will all remain only a pleasant dream, for the Germans seem to have been destined never to be treated in accordance with their own characteristics. The Germans have to have foreign standards forced on them, because those who could change this situation so seldom have the heart to be as they truly are—for what would the neighbors say if one wanted to treat the Germans as German!

So, the doctor said, let us congratulate ourselves anew on our fortunate situation in which we can spend our days in continual traffic with nature without thereby being cut off from the world. I have seen the most beautiful cloisters in the world. I have often been moved by a longing for the contemplative life that seems to pass so eternally and peacefully in places such as on Monte Cassino, in the woods of Camadoli, and in the beautiful cloisters by the Main and the Rhine. But I always changed my mind when I noticed how far away from nature that whole way of life leads, how a tediousness and even disgust towards nature came about as a consequence of the self-torment that is imposed upon the committed as a strict law. Out of all possible orders there is only one I wish to be maintained, one that appears to me to fill a need in human society. It is the Carthusian Order.[7] Under this order's statutes so many people have been able to continue lives that would otherwise have become quite unbearable. It is the only sanctuary for those who are truly unfortunate, for those who have a hasty deed or error to bewail to which the enthusiasm of youth or social circumstances drove them, and whose consequences are dreadful and can no longer be rectified. The world and its hustle and bustle that takes anyone in its grip who doesn't cut himself off from it, the very participation therein that awakens their fate would break their heart. Life itself would be a humiliation to them had they not already entered a place of peace and seclusion here, a place similar to the one to which we go after death, where the pain about what is irrevocable fades into melancholy and into a general recognition [26] that there is no longer anything desirable in life for the person who has overcome it and a recognition that the fate of a mortal person is above all a sad one. Nowhere have I made more interesting acquaintances than in the Carthusian cloisters, particularly those in France; nowhere have I gained a more profound look into human life and its manifold intricacies. What refuge other than the grave would remain open to him who was so unfortunate as to have been blamed for a wrong he did not do, and thereby to have forfeited his happiness in life, if this charitable society didn't open its arms to him. Underneath its outward appearance of sheer austerity, this society nurtures the most benevolent intentions. It is where life, as it were, flows timelessly by and the quiet existence of the plants is the only existence in which the cloisters' members still take an active part, holding up to them a lasting picture of calmness and seclusion. I even learned a lot about my own craft from the members of this order, for by observing generally, and plants in particular, over a long period of time they have learned about the wonderful relationships plants have to people.

It is true, I said, I have often been surprised at how much you achieved with things that appeared to be minor and inconsequential and that appeared to bear absolutely no relation to the danger of the situation.

—and just because of that, he added, I couldn't have used them in a city where people are best acquainted with the most dangerous remedies and where they have no belief in those simple things.

Thus, Clara said, would you have thereby preferred a residence in a small country village to one in a city?

Not just as a consequence of that, he answered. The natural scientist belongs in the country. I have learned more about physics from the farmers than from the academics' lecture halls. Observation is still the best. How much there is to observe from early morning right up to the complete silence of nightfall outside, from living through one long summer's day, whose end one does not think one will live to see. Here I have observed things about the most universal effects of nature; I have observed things about light, sound, the role of water on the earth and in the clouds, the coming and going of natural forces; I have watched animal life, [27] but in particular I have observed things about plants that no academic could have told me. Whosoever does not see natural life as a whole, who doesn't come to understand its language in its very details, also does not know the extent to which the human body is itself truly a smaller nature within a larger one, a smaller nature that has unbelievably many analogies and links to the larger—links that no one would think to exist had observation and application not taught us that it is so.

I am often terrified of these links, Clara said here, and of the thought that everything is related to man. Indeed, if another power within me didn't balance out this horror of nature, I would die from the thought of this eternal night and retreat of light, of this eternally struggling beingness that never actively is. Only the thought of God makes our inner being light and peaceful again.

At that very moment the lights of a nearby house not far from her home shone into the carriage that itself came to a stop just a few minutes later. Theresa went up with Clara and we others all went our own ways home.

II

We had noticed that since her return our friend had a strong and almost continual desire to talk about things concerning that other world. The events of the time, infected with a peculiar sorrow, were suggestive of an even darker future and had made the beautiful soul lose the peaceful demeanor we used to see in her. Her grief about what had happened transformed itself into an inexpressible longing for the future. At the same time there was something forceful in the way in which she strove to go beyond nature and beyond what was real. Ideas about the hidden powers of nature, which had already taken root in her even when in her parental home, and then afterward her friendship with Albert—whose passionate love of certain natural operations linked him to the doctor and, I always suspected, had linked them even earlier—may have [28] filled her with a feeling that within nature there was something nameless and frightful; something toward which, with a dreadful desire, she sometimes felt drawn and sometimes repelled. Neither of us could hide the inherent danger of this condition from ourselves and we agreed that the following day we would, where possible, direct her thoughts along a gentler course, without directly interfering with her current inclinations.

We don't often treat knowledge with indifference, I said at one point, as if there could be an idea within us that would not affect us or have consequences for us. For how many people does a piece of knowledge that contravenes their moral values become a poison; a poison that makes them explode or burst with anger by painfully exciting the mass of impurities within them. Like others, I have seen a striving for knowledge spring from that for which the person is not yet prepared. Perhaps each nature needs its own appropriate insight, an insight with which it alone can feel happy.

I believe, the doctor said, our friend finds herself trapped in just such a process. We just need to keep the crisis under control and steer it towards a healthier goal. What has happened has completely shaken her previous ideas; something unconsciously sleeping within her has been wakened; the views she held no longer help her with this feeling that has stirred in her innermost being; she won't rest until she forms a new world for herself suited to the measure of her feelings. Nothing here stops of its own accord and to some extent we can rely on the strength of her nature.

And so it was that we imagined her condition. An indication of her earlier concern with thoughts of death and the beyond—but, at the same time, also of a remaining peaceful mood and untroubled gaiety therein—was found among her papers after her death. A sheet of paper, unfortunately only a scrap, written by a young and delicate hand, read thus:

[empty place in Schelling's manuscript][1]

[29] There wasn't anything else. When we fetched her during the next few beautiful days of late summer for a walk in the fresh air, she insisted on taking a path that ran through a kind of narrow valley between two hills until there were only two separate tracks, one going up each hill.

When we were on the path, she said:

I feel better here in this little, old vale. Autumn cannot take too much away from it. It keeps the warmth of the sun better and could even make us believe that times were still good. Here the fragrant thyme is still pushing through and intensifies our memory; in the meadow lilies [*die Zeitlose*] have already been swaying for some time, their light blue suggesting the pale color of remembrance, where everything finally disappears.[2] It is supposed to be a poisonous plant. That is where everything finishes, and whatever nature had at the beginning must, indeed, be revealed at the end. Nature, too, seems to have a secret, consuming poison within herself; but why does she share it with her children, so that even they become consumed by it?

I find your complaint unjust, the doctor responded. Even in your own opinion nature is suffering from a hidden poison that she would like to overcome or reject, but cannot. Doesn't she mourn with us? We are able to complain, but she suffers in silence and can talk to us only through signs and gestures. What a quiet sorrow lies in so many flowers, the morning dew, and in the evening's fading colors. In only few of her appearances does nature emerge as terrible, and then always only temporarily. Soon everything retreats into its usual confines and in her normal life nature appears always as a subjugated strength that moves us through the beauty that it brings forth when in this condition.

It's true, she replied. For example, I don't know why for me some flowers hold so sweet a sorrow in their fragrance, and I always have to conclude that the flower must itself have that same sorrow for it to smell like that.

[30] For me, too, I said, nature's whole being or essence seems to testify that she isn't voluntarily subjected to this condition and that she longs to be released from transience. What is frightening about nature is that nothing lasts; that inner necessity that in the end destroys everything—a necessity that is all the more hideous, the quieter it is. Where does this indiscriminate, never-ending force of death lead? Philosophers may very well say: there is no death, nothing in itself fades away; here they assume an arbitrary explanation of death and dying. However, what we others call it still remains, nevertheless, and words can no more explain this than they can explain it away.

This, too, is always a bad way out, the doctor said. But this terrible reality of death doesn't justify people's complaints about nature; people should look to themselves first!

What a thought! Clara responded.

A thought, he answered, that I hope to make clear to you, if you will only answer a few questions for me.

With pleasure, she answered.

Now then, he asked, what do you understand by the very concept of nature? Without doubt you think of it as an essentially creative force?

Above all, she said.

A force, then, that in its essence is concerned only with creation?

Of course, she answered.

Which, therefore, can never in itself be concerned with destruction?

Why not? she countered. For it seems that the very force that creates is also that which destroys.

I asked, he responded, whether that force *in itself* would ever be concerned with destruction and I consider this to be impossible. Rather, as long as the creative force is unconstricted and free, it will carry on satisfying its pure pleasure in creating. However, if it came up against a resistant material that let itself be formed only up to a certain point and that therefore limited the force's pleasure in creating, the force would [31] abandon or even intentionally destroy this material just to carry on enjoying its pleasure in creating, even if it also knew that with the next creation it would come up against the same point again.

That's likely, she said in reply.

Now then, he continued, the basis on which the creative force becomes a destructive one doesn't lie in the creative force itself, and, thus, nor does the basis of destruction either, but lies in something foreign, in something that has come into it, in a restriction or limitation.

Certainly, she answered.

Thus, in itself, he said, nature would be innocent of destruction?

That's certainly how it appears, she said.

Now then, he said, both for Himself and in accordance with His nature, isn't God supposed to be able to be the originator of death, and doesn't it hold in an even higher sense for Him than for nature that He takes pleasure in constructing but not in destroying, and in creating rather than annihilating?

Undeniably, she said.

But apart from God and nature, what remains? he asked further.

I can see exactly where you are going, she said in reply; that what remains stands between God and nature and that this is man. However, you know that inferences like these never satisfy me. I can't make sense of anything that I can't see developing and coming into being right before my eyes.

Very well, then, he said, I will continue by means of narration, after I have asked you two more questions. You agree that nature is to be contrasted with the spirit world?

She agreed.

And that we can regard man as the turning point between the two worlds?

Here, too, she agreed.

So, he continued, shouldn't we suppose that a divine law prescribed that nature should rise up first to man in order to find within him the point at which the two worlds are unified; that afterwards the one should immediately [32] merge with the other through him, the growth of the external world continuing uninterrupted into the inner or spirit world? For, indeed, a transition also occurs now with everything, or at least man when he dies, going over into the spirit world. But this transition happens only indirectly through death and through a complete separation from nature, so that neither the former nor the latter life is able to call itself a whole, for each is only a side of the whole or of the undivided one. But at that other time there would have been no death, in my opinion. Man would have lived both a spiritual and bodily life at the same time, even here; the whole of nature would have risen to heaven or to an enduring and eternal life in and with man. God did not want a lifeless or necessary tie (between the external and inner world), but a free and living one, and man bore the word of this link in his heart and on his lips. Thus the whole of nature's elevation, too, depended on man's freedom. It rested on whether he would forget what was behind him and reach toward what lay before him. Now, however, man reached back (*how* this happened and why God permitted it, I do not ask); man even called for and hankered back to this external world, and by stopping not only his own progress, but that of the whole of nature, he thereby lost the heavenly world. Whoever has seen with their own eyes what terrible consequences a constricted development has on the human body, a development that nature strongly desires; whoever has seen how a crisis in an illness remains, due to an inept treatment or to a weakness already present, making the crisis unmanageable, and how such a crisis immediately causes the body's strength to relapse to a mortal frailty unfailingly resulting in death; whoever has seen this will be able to get a general idea of the destructive effects that the constriction of evolution suddenly entering in through man must have had on the whole of nature. The strength that had emerged fully and powerfully, ready to rise up into a higher world and to reach its point of transfiguration, withdrew back into the present world and consequently suffocated the inner drive toward life. This drive, though still like a fire enclosed within, now acted as [33] a fire of pain and fear looking everywhere for an outlet because it was no longer possible for it to rise up. Any stage leading upward is delightful, but the one that has fallen is frightful. Doesn't everything point to a life that has sunk downward? Have these hills grown just as they stand here? Has the ground that carries us come about by rising up or by sinking back? And, in addition, surely it's not that a stable, constant order prevails here, but that chance, too, set in once the lawful development had been constricted? Or who will believe that the waters that so obviously have had an effect everywhere, that have severed these valleys and have left behind so many sea creatures in our hills, are the result of everything working in accordance with an inner law? Who will suppose that a divine hand has laid hard stone on top of slippery clay, so that the rocks would subsequently slide down and bury in terrible ruins not only the peaceful valleys dotted with people's homes, but also the walkers happily going their way?[3] Oh, the true ruins are not those of ancient human splendor that the curious seek out in the Persian or Indian deserts; the whole Earth is one great ruin, where animals live as ghosts and men as spirits and where many hidden powers and treasures are locked away as if by an invisible strength or by a magician's spell. And we wanted to blame these powers that are locked up rather than thinking about freeing them within us first? Certainly, in his own way man is no less spellbound and transformed. Because of this, heaven sent higher beings from time to time, who were supposed to undo the spell within his inner being and to open up to him a glance into the higher world again with their wonderful hymns and magic charms. Most people, however, are completely captivated by external appearances and think that it is therein that it is to be found. Just as farmers creep round an old, destroyed, or enchanted castle with divining rods in their hands, or shine their lamps into chambers buried underground, and even go with crowbars and levers in the hope of finding gold or other valuables:[4] so, too, does man go about nature, entering some of her [34] hidden rooms and calling this search "natural science." But the treasures are not covered by rubble alone; the treasures have been locked up in the very wreckage and rocks themselves by a spell that only another magic charm can undo.[ii]

With this speech we had got to the point where the path stopped. Clara seemed to be tired and she sat down on the stone bench in the ground, which a talented mason had made out of the nearby breakage. Until now the sun had been on our backs, but as we turned round, the sun was now to the side of the opening of the small valley, thus casting this side in shadow. The intense illumination of the other side heightened the wonderful impression of the irregular masses of rock and the many thick bushes with autumnal red and dun leaves that were pushing through the rock. Now and again, from one of the apple trees that were behind the bench and that stretched all the way up the steep hill like a forest, the movement of the air lifted a withered leaf and gently laid it on Clara's lap or in her hair. She didn't seem to notice; it then occurred to me how different it was in spring last year when she sat under these trees and they showered her with their blossoms.

In the meantime the doctor came back, having gone up the bank to gather some of the berries that preserve some sweetness only through the cold and frost of the autumn nights. Clara turned to him and said: You have given me a clarification [*Licht*] I desired.[5] I have suspected such a magical connection of man to nature for a long time. That's why all creatures look to him, for everything counts on man. Everything seems to recriminate him with hushed sighs or to turn on him as the common enemy. Justifiably are all of nature's arrows aimed at him. Justifiably does the cold, destructive north wind rage against him in one direction, while in the other a poisonous wind rises up from the desert, which consumes his life strength. Justifiably do his dwellings collapse over his head when the Earth

---

ii. Marginal note by F. W. J. Schelling: A completely different world buried therein than we suspected. Odyssey of the Spirit.

[35] shudders from the strength of the fire enclosed within; justifiably does the erupting stream of fire devastate his painstaking work with wild abandon. When the strength that was ready to develop within the animal kingdom was driven back into inner being, that strength transformed itself into an enflamed anger or poison, and it justifiably turned against man first of all.

But, the doctor said, interrupting her, just think of nature's many bright and beneficent strengths. She still hasn't forgotten that through man she shall be raised up further and freed, that even now the talisman still lies within him through which she will be redeemed. That is why she comes to man in thanks when he scatters seeds on the earth, tills and waters the wild and arid ground, and why she rewards him with extravagant abundance. It seems to me that her feeling for man is essentially one of friendship and often of sympathy—

And yet, she broke in, nature passes so heartlessly over scenes of sorrow and despair. A poor creature is lying exhausted with a feverish temperature, thirsting for the refreshment and help that a cool breeze could bring, but mercilessly the sun sends down its strongest rays, the air and the earth condensing them to a stifling heat. Elsewhere someone is driven from house and home, leaving behind his wife and children grieving after him in despair; the heavens send him down rain and storms, and hail hits the exposed head of the one despised.

This unfortunate person, the doctor said, interrupting once again, will find nature more in agreement with him in this instance than if she were to compliment him with fresh air and sweet sunshine. He may be deceiving himself, like those who believe that nature smiles on their day of joy. For on her great path to the common good nature can perhaps only seldom take part in the fate and mood of an individual. But perhaps important changes have never happened in whole nations without there being a general shift in nature at the same time. History books are full of this; how many signs from heaven, in the air and on earth, have presaged these [36] fateful times. Everything speaks to us and would so much like to make itself understood. Many are well disposed to man and manifestly have the will to bring him tidings of his near future, if he wanted to hear. I could even quote some perhaps quite incredible observations in support of this.

It is only too true, she replied, everything presses itself on man either with hostility or in friendship, everything seeks him alone and would like to seize what is his. That's why man can't resist the spellbinding sight of gold, worldly enticements, or the attractions of earthly beauty. Nothing leaves him feeling indifferent, everything moves him—

Because *he* should move everything, the doctor broke in, because he is not conscious of the strength in his inner being through which he could rule everything and through which he could be free of everything. Sloth and churlishness are man's worst enemies and are a consequence of that first Fall. Whoever does not take hold of himself will before long take hold of something else. Whoever does not want to go onward, sinks back. And evil consists even now in a backward motion of human nature, which, instead of wanting to raise itself up into its true being, always clings onto and attempts to realize what should be only a condition of its activity and only a quiet, immobile basis of its life. What causes illness other than a churlishness toward development, other than the individual strength not wanting to continue with the whole, not wanting to die away with the whole, but obstinately wanting to be for itself? Consequently, we should strive against this condition more than anything else. The person who is roused is not lost. God helps the active and forgives them much. It is incredible how much being active is worth in and of itself.

I know that inner strength, Clara said, getting up to go back, and I have found that it can raise us above everything external; but I also know that before it even knows it, the best inner being gets tied up in a contradiction with the external world.

Even this, the doctor said, is the necessary consequence of that first [37] sinking back. Although everything that is high and divine can rise up out of the world as a flower rises up from the earth, once the world has been fixed as one that is external, something nevertheless remains in it that is foreign, something for which the world is merely its bearer and that the world is unable to receive into itself. The prevailing law is concerned only with upholding this foundation; everything else is and must be accidental to it.

And above all, she said, is man likewise incidental to it, too. The holiest necessity of my inner being is not a law for nature. In nature even divine necessity takes on the color and appearance of chance, and what was initially accidental operates with the irresistible force of a terrible necessity once present. If only it were at least possible to keep our inner being free of this contradiction! But just there the contradiction manifests its greatest power. It forces us to mistrust our heart's tenderest feelings. We are beings who do not love without being punished; and, in contrast, the law of our inner being would be capable of requiring actions that any human, feeling heart would surely have to abhor. I see enough even within the simplest, elementary, and most irrefutable things to verify my feeling that not only do and will terrible things occur, they *must* do so.

It is our duty, the doctor said, to recognize just this. Looking away or closing your eyes just to avoid seeing this condition doesn't help. As humans we may like to complain about the downfall of the most beautiful and lovely things in the world; but at the same time we should consider each such fall with a kind of quiet joy, because it holds a confirmation of the view that we must have of this world and is our most immediate reference to another, higher world. How much happier most people would be, how much pointless longing would come to an end, how much easier would life be borne and relinquished, if everyone continually kept in mind that here anything divine is only appearance and not reality, that even whatever is most spiritual isn't free, but arises only conditionally—that it is the blossom and here and there even the fruit, but not the trunk and the roots.

[38] Yet most, or even all, people do say that, Clara responded.

They certainly say that, he replied, but they think it could be otherwise and blame man, and for this reason they would also like to sever all man's connections to nature. Their systems and views thereby get just as confused as their moral doctrines. They start with what is most general and spiritual and are thereby never able to come down to reality or particulars. They are ashamed to start from the earth, to climb up from the creature as if from a rung on a ladder, to draw those thoughts that are beyond the senses first from earth, fire, water, and air. And so they don't get anywhere, either: their webs of thought are plants without roots, they don't hang onto anything, like spiders' webs do on shrubs or walls; instead, they float in the air and the sky like these delicate threads here in front of us. And yet they believe they can strengthen man thereby, even help advance the age that nevertheless suffers by the very fact that while one part has indeed sunk completely into the mud, the other has presumed to climb so high that it can no longer find the ground beneath it. If we want everything that is spiritual to be in this world, what do we have left for a future one? And it seems to me as man stood here on earth in this life, with his strong, firm bones, in bygone times he had a completely different and far more definite idea about that other life. Only he who already knows his opposite through and through can look the spiritual right in the eye; just as only he is to be called "free" who knows what is necessary and the conditions under which he can prevail. Man must first develop and grow even to get to freedom; and even freedom rises up in this world from necessity's obscurity, bursting forth only in its last appearance as inexplicable, divine, as a flash of eternity that splits up the darkness of this world, but that is also immediately devoured by its very own effect.

I have often thought, Clara said in reply, that the sight of freedom—not the freedom that is usually so-called, but the true [39] and real one—would have to be unbearable to man, even though people talk about it continually and praise it at every instant. They are so satisfied with determining the grounds or even the basic principles for all their actions and then portraying this progeny of their heart as freedom. And I don't know if I am mistaken, but it seems to me that of all kinds of freedom this one is at least of the very lowest order. A female friend of mine used to say: heaven is freedom. But if freedom is heaven, then it must also be unbounded, complete, and divine freedom.

I am completely of the same opinion, the doctor responded. Most people are scared of freedom as they are of magic, of anything that can't be explained, and of the spirit world in particular. Freedom is the true and actual appearance of spirit; that's why the appearance of freedom brings man down; the world bows to it. But so few know how to handle this delicate secret; that's why we see that those to whom the capacity falls to use this divine right become like madmen and, gripped by the madness of caprice, they try to prove freedom in actions that lack the character of internal necessity and that are thereby those that are the most accidental. Necessity is the inner being of freedom; thus, no basis can be found to truly free action; freedom is as it is because it is so, it just is, it is absolutely and thereby necessarily. But freedom such as this is not of this world. Thus, those who deal with the world can seldom exert such freedom, if at all. These people must surrender themselves to art instead; for in the decided mastery of the external, what is innermost—and, indeed, the more internal it is, the more it takes on the appearance of something external—must seem to serve to help itself to be tolerated. Such was God's will, it appears, with everything first becoming as external as possible, and the inner life becoming manifest only by coming through with the hardest struggle and the most powerful opposition. The more we recognize the limitations of this world, the holier we will find each appearance of something higher and better within it to be. We will never [40] demand it passionately; but where it is naturally, where we meet a heart that has heaven within it or a soul that is a quiet temple of heavenly revelation or an activity or a work that shows the internal and external reconciled through divine leniency, such things we will embrace with loving strength. We will consider them holy and honor them as signs of a world in which the external is subordinated to the internal, as the internal is here to the external.

Oh, leave us, Clara said, turning back once more toward the sinking sun, turn your gaze to these regions; for now that high, holy, spiritual realm is nearer to me than nature, world, and life.

We went in silence through the gate and escorted her through the small street to the other gate until we reached her house.

III

The days quickly became unpleasant and were not suited to long walks.

I watched our friend, and I could see that she was always occupied with one thing.

A wonderful depth of feeling that could enter right into her way of thinking betrayed itself in some conversations; however, what she lacked was the ability to unpack her thoughts and thereby clarify them. I know what an agreeable effect ordering one's own thoughts into a precise framework has; the soul is happy when it can have what it felt inwardly, as if by inspiration or through some divine thought, expressly worked out in the understanding, too, as if looking in a mirror. Profound souls shy away from this development, which they see as one in which they have to come out of themselves. They always want to go back into their own depths [*ihre eigne Tiefe*] and to continue to enjoy the bliss of the center.

I decided that first of all I would counteract this tendency in our friend and that I would use the first opportunity to do so. I was convinced that [41] once we have made up our minds to unpack our thoughts, we usually find everything even more marvelous and wonderful than we had imagined.

Meanwhile she got there first with her own request.

It was on Christmas Eve, when she had invited my children round so that she could give them a surprise present and for this one day to act where possible as a replacement for the mother they had lost.

This whole evening there was something transfigured about her and a sort of indescribable cheerfulness in her that we had not seen for a long time. After the children's first rush of excitement was over and the older girls had sat to one side, one of whom had been given the poems that she'd wanted for a long time and the other the drawings, she drew back to the end [*die Tiefe*] of the room; and once we'd sat down she started to say:

The sight of these well-behaved children brings back to you and me both the image of their mother, whom I didn't know, and this gives me the most pronounced [*klarste*] certainty that she is, that she lives, and that she's taking part in our happiness.[1] To me, it's as if this day brings the departed ones closer to us; for didn't this day once join Earth again to heaven?

Certainly, I said; for angels had to celebrate this birth and proclaim God in the highest and peace on Earth, because what is above had come back to what is below and because the chain that had been broken for so long was joined again.

In moments like this, she continued, my conviction needs no reason; I see everything as if it were present. To me, it feels as if the spirit life were already embracing even me, as if I were still strolling on Earth but as a completely different kind of being, as one borne by a soft, gentle element, as if I were without need and without pain—why can't we hold onto these moments?

Perhaps, I said in reply, this level of profundity isn't compatible with the limitations of our present life, whose destiny appears to be such that everything will be explained and recognized only bit by bit. [42] And isn't it so, I added, that when you are in such a state it seems as if your whole being were unified in One focal point, as if it were one light, one flame?

That's just how I feel, she said.

And when you come out of this state, do you feel unhappy?

At least far less happy, she said.

And, I continued, you can't prevent yourself from coming out of this state?

She said that it happened against her will.

Therefore, I said, a necessity must indeed lie within the alternation of these states as in other alternations of this kind. That experience of the center, which floods us with a feeling of the greatest well-being, doesn't seem appropriate for the mediocrity of our present life. We must regard it as an extraordinary privilege, but we mustn't despise the ordinary state as a consequence.

But with what should we fill the comparative emptiness? she responded.

With activity, I answered, or actually by procuring the goods from that higher state for this one, too.

And how could that be possible? she asked.

It's not impossible, I said, for us to piece back together again what we saw directly in, as it were, a united way; and thus, from the knowledge that lies within each individual piece, finally to create a whole similar to what we occasionally felt and which we can then enjoy when this blissful view is taken away from us. And just this development of knowledge, which elevates that knowledge to science, seems to me to be man's true spiritual destiny for this life.

I've always felt the respect for science, she said, that someone feels for something that is denied them but from which they nevertheless see wonderful results. For you yourself know [43] how much trust I've always placed in you as a man of science, as someone from whom, I was firmly convinced, I could always get spiritual advice. A certain confidence, reliability, and constancy seem to be able to exist only in science. But I will respect it twice as much if it has the magic power to retain the bliss of the contemplative state.

But I don't say that it can do that, I replied. The feeling that science gives is another; it is quieter, more even, and more constant. However, what I did say is that even if that knowledge is at its very clearest and indescribably real, it is temporary in spiritual intuition; and science only shows that knowledge to the soul as if it were retaining it as a faithful memory and making it truly our own for the first time.

And, she asked again, how is this retention effected?

Through clear concepts, I answered, in which what was known in an indivisible way is taken to pieces or separated and then made into a unity again.

So a separation must happen first? she said.

Of course, I answered; and you can see for yourself how necessary this is if we are also to ensure that what was immediately understood is procured as an abiding good. For it would certainly be foolish still to want *proofs* to come to your aid in procuring the immediate certainty of life after death for yourself, for proofs only ever produce a merely indirect insight. But didn't you once say yourself: you require the immortality of the whole person?

I did say that, she answered.

How necessary, then, it is for us partially to differentiate and, as it were, to place before us everything that pertains to the whole person so that we know what we mean when we say the phrase "the whole person." So shall we examine this a bit further?

She agreed.

Good, I said. Then you will certainly count the body, too, as belonging to the whole person? [44]

Certainly, she said.

And as well as the body, there is also the spirit?

Of course, she replied.

And do you suppose that the spirit is the same as the body or that it is different from or even opposed to it?

The latter, she answered.

But how do you suppose that these two opposites can be united into a single whole?

Only through a truly divine tie does this seem to me to be possible, she answered.

Now, shan't we also look for the word for this tie? It must be present within us insofar as each of us, too, is a whole person?

Without a doubt, she said.

So it must also be known to us?

Naturally.

And as that which connects, it must share equally in the nature of both the things it connects?

So it seems.

Thus it must be something mediate between body and spirit?

Of course.

And not be as sharply opposed to the body as the spirit is, but it must be, as it were, a milder essence that, so to speak, touches the spirit with its upper part but descends right down to the body with its lower part, merging into material being?

This too seemed to be clear to her.

Now, what will we call this essence that is by nature moderate and mild and that is present in us?

She indicated that she could not guess.

Astonishing, I said, for it is so close to us. So, I continued, don't we say that people who have excellent minds have a spirit?

Of course. [45]

And who are these people?

Those, she opined, who occupy themselves mostly with spiritual matters and who demonstrate a great strength in this respect.

But, I continued, is it ever the spirit in and for itself that we love, that wins the trust of our heart?

It doesn't appear to me to be so, she said, for very often the spirit in itself has something rather repellent about it, and, although we recognize it with respect, we do not approach it with trust.

Isn't it precisely what we find human in people, I continued, that we usually take to our heart?

Certainly, she said.

So, spirit wouldn't be what is actually human in people?

It wouldn't to me, she said.

So what would it be, then?

I admit, she said, that I don't see where your questions are leading.

But you remember that we said that some people have a lot of spirit, just as we could say of others that they are very physical. Now, isn't there a third a class of person?

Indeed, she said, now I understand. Of other people we say that they have a soul.

And it is just this that we love above all; that draws us, as it were, in a magical way, so that we immediately give our trust to those of whom we say in this respect that they have soul.

That is how it is, she confirmed.

The soul would therefore be what is actually human in man, too?

Certainly, she said.

And, thus, it would also be that gentle, moderate essence between body and spirit?

She acknowledged this, too.

And, thus, the whole person would actually be a whole made up of the three: body, spirit, and soul? [46]

That's how it is, she said.

But, I continued, how can we conceive of linking these three into a whole?

That would certainly be a hard question to answer, she said.

We will see, I said. Whatever independently unites two opposites should certainly be of a higher kind than those other two?

That's how it seems.

The soul should therefore be of a higher lineage than spirit and body?

She agreed with this as well.

And yet, I said, in being, as it were, closer to the body than the spirit is, the soul appears to be placed lower down relative to the spirit.

It appeared to her to be like that, too.

Are we able to say at all, of any of the three, that one alone is exclusively that which links the others, I asked further, and doesn't each one become the means again of linking the others? The spirit merges into the body through the soul, but through the soul the body is raised once again into the spirit. The soul is connected to the spirit only insofar as a body is there at the same time, and it is connected to the body only insofar as the spirit is there at the same time; for if either of them were missing, it could not possibly be present as a unity, i.e., as a soul. The whole person thus represents a kind of living rotation: wherever one thing reaches into the other, neither of the others can leave, each requires the other.

A wonderful concept, she said in reply, with which I must also agree.

And yet, I said, out of these three the soul has an advantage.

What may that be? she asked.

If, I answered, the body were posited quite purely and for itself, would the spirit also necessarily be posited thereby?

It appears not, she said, for they are opposites.

And if the spirit were posited in such a way, would the body necessarily be posited? [47]

That, too, just as little, she said.

But if the soul were posited, would body and spirit also necessarily be posited thereby?

That's how it is, she said.

The soul would thus indeed be the *most noble* of the three,[iii] because it alone includes the other two within it; these latter, however, including neither their opposite nor the soul within themselves?

She agreed with this, too.

Thus, when we were speaking about a survival of the whole person, I said, we wouldn't have been satisfied with a survival merely of the body?

Certainly not, she answered.

Nor with a survival merely of the spirit?

Nor that.

But if someone could give us a firm assurance of the survival of the soul, we would be comforted?

It at least seems as if we could be, she answered.

I certainly would be for my part, I responded, and I would tell that person as much. If a clairvoyant had said to me in my twentieth year that I would live for

---

iii. Marginal note by F. W. J. Schelling: The innermost germ of all, which will actually come to light through the other two.

another thirty years, I wouldn't have understood this as meaning that the body I had then was to remain the same for thirty years, for of course I knew that even after twenty years of material existence my body had become completely different from how it was at the start. Nor would I have believed that my spirit would remain the same, for my spirit had gained completely different convictions and from the very beginning had such varying views, even in the short time I had lived. Rather, I would have thought that although body and spirit may undergo many changes, what had been myself from the very beginning—what seemed to me and to others to remain always the same and which they loved or hated about me through all the changes—[48] would always remain the same even after thirty years of changes. But you say that my soul will live forever, and I don't understand this as meaning that neither my body nor my spirit could undergo the greatest changes. Rather, I understand it as meaning that what would live eternally would be just that innermost being, my own self that was neither body nor spirit, but which was the uniting consciousness of both; that is, it was the soul that would live eternally. Haven't we already gained a lot, I asked her, in having worked out what it actually is that is said to continue to live when people say that there is survival after death, and that this is, namely, (the actual innermost germ of life) nothing other than the soul?

Indisputably, she answered.

And don't we see that philosophers haven't done too badly at all in always preferring to talk about the immortality of the soul, as if just therein everything were to be gained, even if perhaps they didn't always exactly know why?

Nevertheless, I do still have some doubts, she answered.

Now, I said, it's your turn to ask the questions, for I have already overstepped my turn.

What causes me to doubt, she began, is this. If we have saved the soul from decline, then it certainly appears that this must intrinsically hold for body and spirit, too, because we have supposed that the soul is the unity of them both. But I fear that someone could turn this on its head and say: if body and spirit are separated at death—and this certainly does have to be assumed—then intrinsically their tie would be dissolved, too, because either those that were previously linked no longer exist at all or one or both of them do survive, but separately. But here is what appears to me to be an even greater difficulty: namely, we said that what actually survives is the soul and yet everyone, including ourselves, in common agreement, calls the world into which we are transported after death the "spirit world," and thus we prefer to think of our departed ones as spirits. [49]

In truth, I replied, you have understood everything excellently. May I, too, succeed in completely unraveling anything that remains obscure. And it is quite true that we have spoken about the soul as the tie between spirit and body in a very imprecise way, particularly because at times we spoke as if there could indeed be a body for itself and a spirit for itself at some point. For if this were possible, we couldn't deny that their tie could be severed. But as soon as we had mentioned these three, didn't we realize that each would require the other, that none of them could dispense with the other, and that, therefore, once they were together they would be chained to each other by a completely unbreakable tie?

Certainly, she said.

I asked further: didn't we imagine their relationship to each other to be a living rotation in which one always reaches into the other, so that either all of them have to stop being at the same time or, if one survives, they must necessarily all survive?

That's how it was, she said.

But now for life's present rotation, at least, they are chained to each other in this way?

Certainly, she said.

And not in a chance way, but essentially so, such that if you take one of them away, you take all of them?

She agreed.

Now, I asked further, couldn't I offer a completely different proof of survival from this interconnection—as philosophers used to offer a proof of survival from the simplicity of the soul—if it is a proof as such that we are interested in here?

So it would seem, she said, if only death did not so obviously remove a link from the rotation; for if they can exist only together, then together they must also fall.

That's just what I wanted to avoid, my dear. For see whether what you've assumed here is so certain, whether it is as undeniable as it appears to be to most people [50] who thus regard death as a complete rending and separation of spirit and soul from the body and likewise of the body from them. For, supposing it were like this at the end, as thinking people we couldn't just immediately assume this from appearances. And, so, above all else we would have to ask what death is and what change is brought about by it within the present life's rotation. This also touches upon what you said before as your second point: namely, that it seems that although it is the soul that actually survives, everyone talks about that other life as a spirit life. Or wasn't this how it was?

That's how it was, she said.

And certainly it seems surprising, not only for that reason, but also how we are quite generally led to imagine the condition that follows our present one as a spiritual one at all, almost as if it were through a prior agreement or some kind of natural disposition. For if they wanted to assume survival, it wouldn't cost them anything to have the departed soul pass straight on to another body, and not even necessarily into an animal's body, as those who teach the transmigration of souls have it, nor even into another person's body, but into a body suited to that soul and without the soul's losing its personality. So what could the reason be for this almost universal view of death; for, in its favor, we may certainly consider that opinion as offering a positive concept of death, instead of a purely negative one in which death is supposed to consist of a separation of the soul from the body?

That death is represented as a positive transition into a spiritual condition, and not simply as the end of the present condition, already seems to me to be a great gain, she said. But if we don't want to look to our religious teachings for the universality of this idea, then I don't know the reason for it. We would presumably have to say that it is natural for people to think of any condition in which a transition occurs through leaving a previous condition as being that condition's opposite.

And, I said in response, this explanation seems to me to be quite justified. [51] So, they surely also supposed that man's present condition is the corporeal condition?

Of course.

And, yet, in this bodily condition the whole person is present; not just the body, but also the spirit and the soul?

Naturally.

And even within corporeality the soul is what is the essence or what is actually human about a person?

That, too, is what's supposed, she said.

But from this condition man passes onto the opposite one and, thus, onto a spiritual condition?

Certainly.

And the person is still the whole person, even in this spiritual condition?

I don't know if they meant it like that, she said.

And yet, I answered, they must have meant it like that. For, according to their way of thinking, death was nothing other than a transition from the corporeal condition into a spiritual one. But there would be no reason why anything should go missing from the whole person in this transition if, despite the corporeality of the prior condition, the whole person—that is, body, spirit, and soul—were present. Or, which is the more astonishing: that even in the spiritual condition the person stays together as body, soul, and spirit, that is, as a whole person; or that in the corporeal condition the person was not just a body, but also both spirit and soul at the same time?

Of course, she said, in itself the former is as astonishing as the latter.

But you remember, I continued, that very recently our friend put forward to me at least a very convincing case that in the present life the soul is bewitched by material existence.

I certainly do remember, she answered.

Now, I continued, if it so happens that even in the present life the soul [52] is completely held fast by the body despite the soul's being what is essential to man, how much more so must it happen that the soul becomes bewitched and held fast by the spirit?

This is certainly very enlightening, she said: only the transfer from the corporeal into the spiritual has yet to be made comprehensible.

Perhaps, I replied, that shall remain a mystery to us until we ourselves have experienced it. However, I can't call it incomprehensible, for such transfers continually occur even within the narrow circle of the present.

And what may they be? she asked.

Well, I said, such as in the transition from wakefulness to sleep and vice versa; life's rotation does not itself stop in sleep, it is just transferred from one medium into another. Or from many signs don't we tend to attribute the spirit as being busy with thoughts, inventions, and other activities in sleep, even if we don't remember them afterwards? And nor does the soul lose the capacity to will, love, or detest in sleep, either.

My friend, she said, it seems that here you are explaining something obscure through something that is just as, or at least almost as, obscure itself.

Yes, you're right, I answered, but for me it all has to do with just one thing: to show how the rotation that is posited by body, spirit, and soul could be transferred without its being raised up from one world into another.

So, she continued, your idea must therefore be that in death the soul is raised up to being a spiritual soul?

Certainly, I said.

And that in the present life it has been only a corporeal soul?

Of course.

But how can you assert this, she said, for even now the soul associates with supernatural and heavenly things?

Oh, I answered, everything is of course contained in everything else: the lower level contains prophecies of the higher, but this level nevertheless still remains [53] the lower one. Even animal life wants to go beyond itself: the beaver constructs its palace in the water with a humanlike understanding; other animals live in humanlike conditions and domestic relationships. So there's a lot that can carry man away into that higher world even now; there are also some people who voluntarily and consciously let what they have to leave behind in death die now and who try as far as possible to live a spiritual life. But the aim here is to determine this life's general level and this cannot be found from those who are predominantly suited to leaving it.

But the body? she responded. If the soul becomes spiritual in that other life, then surely the body does, too?

Of course, I said; yet this doesn't seem to me to be quite the right expression, and only now do I see that we should have expressed ourselves differently in respect of the soul, too.

And how, then? she asked.

We shouldn't have said that the soul becomes spiritual after death, as if it weren't already spiritual before; but that the spiritual, which was already in the soul but seemed to be more tied down there, becomes freed and prevails over the other part through which the soul was closer to the corporeal, the part that rules in this life. So, too, then, we shouldn't say that the body becomes spiritual in that higher life, as if it weren't spiritual from the beginning; but that the spiritual side of the body that here was hidden and subordinate, becomes one that there is manifest and dominant.

So, she said, not only would the soul have two sides, but perhaps the spirit, too, and most certainly the body?

Indisputably, I replied. For even here you surely remember our friend's speech about the earth, and thus the body, too, which is taken from the earth, as having been fated to be not merely external but both external and internal, and that it should be one in both of them; that the appearance of the whole as merely external was the consequence of a delayed development that could not destroy the internal essence, but that could nevertheless [54] entangle, tie, and thus subordinate that essence to the external. Now isn't it natural that if the form of the body where the internal is held fast by the external should disintegrate, the other form, where the external breaks free from and, as it were, overcomes the internal, would become free?

So, she said, this spiritual form of the body must have already been present in the purely external one, too?

Of course, I answered, but as a germ that may often try to move but, in being held down by the force of external life, is able only partly to show its presence and only under particular conditions.

I remember having often heard people talk before about a more subtle body contained in the coarser one, Clara said, and that at death this subtle body parts with the coarser one; only I don't know why this idea always gave me so little satisfaction.[2]

This is the case for any opinion that has been formed purely by chance. Unless something comes to us along with a necessary framework, it can't truly work itself into the soul.

But the very sense behind this view was a completely different one, too, she said.

Of course, for that middle essence was thought of only as a more subtle body, not as a really spiritual form.

But, she continued, is this heavenly germ of life supposed to be within us alone, or merely within all organic beings but not in inorganic ones—or how does this work?

I don't see why the germ of a higher life shouldn't simply be in each and every thing, only more openly in some and more hidden in others, I answered. For the whole of nature was meant to represent the external and the internal in complete harmony. And all creatures, the scriptures say, long with us and as much as we do for the higher life, and it's only that here this latter is more developed in us.

So, she said, shouldn't the presence of that germ really also be represented within all things?

I don't know, I replied, whether we can give such a grand description to the signs of life we now know about in respect of bodies or to the electrical interplay of forces or to chemical transformations, [55] and I don't consider it impossible that a whole new series of such signs would arise if we could change them not just externally, but if we could directly affect that inner germ of life. For I don't know if I'm mistaken or if it's a peculiarity of my way of seeing things, but to me all things, even the most corporeal things, seem as if they were ready to offer up quite different signs of life again from those we know now.

But then all things would die, too? she went on to ask.

So it seems, I said, but I'd like to ask you to explain this further yourself.

Death, she said, is the release of the inner form of life from the external one that keeps it suppressed?

Excellent, I said.

And death is necessary because those two forms of life that couldn't exist together at the same time had to exist one after the other instead, once nature had sunk down into the purely external?

Absolutely right, I said, and you have expressed it so marvelously.

But the two forms of life are in each thing?

That is what we've assumed, I answered.

Now, she said, then all things must die without exception.

This seems to me to be undeniably necessary, too, I said.

But, she continued, don't we really see just such a death, particularly in some chemical changes?

I don't know, I said.

I will never forget, she continued, when I first saw the solubility of metal in acids and I wouldn't believe that a transparent liquid, as colorless as water from a well, contained a solution of silver, or that heavenly blue water contained copper, et cetera, until finally I was convinced by my very own eyes.

Astonishing enough it is, too, I said, and gives us much cause to think about the very nature of corporeality. [56]

Aren't those solutions called "spirits" justifiably, she continued, and isn't this disappearance of the very densest and hardest bodies really a solution of the corporeal into the spiritual, and isn't it thus to be called "death"?

It is certainly something similar, I answered; we see to what heights the most corporeal things can go when a higher spirit, as it were, takes hold of them. But are you also convinced about the restoration of all these things to their initial corporeal condition?[3]

Of course, she replied.

Now, I said, I don't know whether the transformation here is any different from when a part of our body happens to have been burnt and is gradually restored to health by externally applied medication.

But, she continued, don't all corporeal things exhibit a drive to become more spiritual? What else is the fragrance of a flower, and how spiritual must those discharges be from those redolent bodies that survive for years without decaying? Doesn't everything want to become air in order to bond with that pure, holy element, which I would nevertheless prefer to regard as an independent, indivisible essence, an essence whose strength before long transforms all that it receives, however diverse they all may be, and makes everything it receives resemble it.

Even all that, I said, behaves like this and proves that all things strive for a freer, independent existence and that they only unwillingly wear the fetters in which they are caught. But who would like to call death a mere transformation into air? To me death seems to be something much more serious.

So, she said, only organic beings and no others provide us with an instance of death?

I don't know, I said, but this is how it seems to me. We organic beings all have the capacity to die, because we are each ourselves a whole. Other things, however, are only members of a greater whole—that of the Earth. They can certainly be combined and changed in many ways within that whole, as far as the planet's life course permits, [57] but the relief of death, or of the complete release of the spiritual life form, befalls them only when the planet has reached its allotted goal and dies.

At that very moment the doctor came in and interrupted the conversation for a while. I told him what we had been talking about and after he had heard the essentials and had thought for a while, he said: So, a separation surely does occur at death?

To what extent? I answered.

As a separation from the body, obviously.

Of course, I said, but not from the innermost essence of the body, but as a separation from the body insofar as the body is something external and is part of merely external nature.

But during the present life, he said, was the body's spiritual essence already present in the merely external body?

At least as a germ, I answered.

But now it seems to follow that as regards perfection it is the present life that has the edge over the future one, he continued.

How so? I said.

This seems quite clear to me, he answered. For in the present life there's not only the body's spiritual essence, there's also the external body that the future life lacks: thus the present life clearly has the advantage.

What I could reply here seems to me to be so obvious that I hardly like to say it, I said.

Do say it, he answered, for there's nevertheless something here that is obscure.

I mean, then, that you wouldn't call a person who has a lot of things of low value "rich," and that, conversely, you wouldn't call someone "poor" who had only a few things—or even only one sole thing, but one that was of invaluable worth, like a precious stone that far surpassed all others.

Certainly not, he said, yet I do not believe that you consider the external body to be an imperfection or a thing of low worth. [58]

If only we can understand each other, I answered, it will all sort itself out. For surely we both admit that there is a difference in worth between the internal and the external; namely, it seems to me, that the external is merely the beingness of the internal [*das blosse Sein des Inneren*], but that the internal is what actively is within the external [*das Seiende in diesem Aeusseren*]. Or is this not so?

I am quite happy with that, he said.

And what actively is, I continued, recognizes beingness, but the reverse—that beingness cognizes what actively is—does not hold?

This too I admit, he said.

However, all cognition involves positing?

Certainly, he said.
And beingness surely also involves positing?
He seemed to give this some thought.
Well, at least a positing of itself, I said.
To that extent, of course, he said.
But it's a positing that doesn't cognize itself, for we said that it is cognized only by what actively is.
He admitted this.
And so, again, what actively is, I continued, is the positing of that positing?
This follows indisputably—
It is thus something higher or more determined and it is very fittingly called—or, at least, so it seems to me—the higher potency of it?
He admitted this.
Thus, as there is a difference between a higher and a lower potency, I continued, so, too, indeed, would there be a difference between the internal and the external. But I would not thereby consider the external in itself as an imperfection or as something of low value. For what actively is needs beingness, as beingness needs what actively is. Indeed, I even think it may be possible for even this difference to disappear completely.

And how? Clara asked, who had been listening to this conversation attentively.

If, I said, the external were so completely suffused by the internal [59] that it had in itself both what cognizes and what is cognized, and if in turn the internal had the external posited in it in such a way that what cognizes also contained what is cognized within it, and if both of these were at the same time, so that the external so conceived were together with an internal so conceived, then this would, indeed, be called the most blessed and perfect life of all and there would no longer be any difference between the external and the internal, because each would contain the other.

Both agreed with this.

Now, I said, within us as we currently are and also partly within other living beings, although in a much more imperfect way, the external appears to be so well formed that it even contains what cognizes within it and it thereby gains a certain independence. For even animals, to whom we are unable to ascribe any true internality, and those people whom we have to consider in almost the same way, nevertheless can cognize all the time through a kind of external necessity, proving that the external within them itself contains that which cognizes.

They both concurred.

But this doesn't at all apply the other way round, I continued; that is, the internal doesn't have the external posited within it as the external does the internal.

Of course, said Clara.

For if that were so, I said, the external would not so generally contradict the internal. The external would not need experience and painstaking research in order to gain knowledge about things; it would immediately be the internally possible deed, and with one Word it would be a completely blessed, even godlike life.

Neither education nor lessons would be necessary, either, if the external were posited just as originally within the internal as the internal is within the external. For people who hadn't been brought up among humans and who'd lived among animals from an early age would, indeed, completely lack that perfect internality, as some examples have shown?

He confirmed this.

[60] And a lot depends on the sort of company that one keeps from childhood on?

This, too, was conceded.

So, this internality is not something that is present, but is something that is brought up and fostered like a flower in a foreign soil?

Of course, was the reply.

But all striving for knowledge is just a striving to posit the external within us as internal, as far as it's possible?

Just that, they said.

And would this striving be necessary if that perfect internality were already present within us?

Impossible, said Clara.

But the doctor broke in here and said: We seem to be at just the right point here. For that striving for knowledge and that many-faceted other, in which we try as far as possible to make everything external internal, is nevertheless a completely free striving?

Of course, I answered.

And here, too, it's possible for the force of freedom within us to subordinate even the body so much to the internal that we can live a pure and unblemished life.

I agreed with this, too.

So, to a certain extent we can already achieve what will happen to us in the other life here; that is, the subordination of the external to the internal. Aren't all philosophers' speeches full of remarks indicating that he who loves wisdom will work toward death even here; but here we still have the body into the bargain. See for yourself whether the present life doesn't have a clear advantage over the future one.

Dear friend, I answered, each thing does indeed have its own merits that the other does not have, and yet perhaps it isn't thereby more estimable than the latter. For example, riches have certain merits over poverty; but if it is riches that generally make it harder or even impossible to enter the kingdom of truth and if, [61] on the other hand, poverty makes it easier, then no wise man would hesitate to choose poverty. Who can't appreciate the merits of the present life? If it didn't have them who would be able to bear it? But the question always remains: which of its merits is in itself the greatest? To me its greatest merit seems to be that here one can care for and bring up that divine germ within oneself, and so one can partly enjoy the bliss of that other life even here. For without this perfect internality the external life, too, would lose its own true charm, which does not consist in the satisfaction of sensual desires, but in the experience of beauty and of inwardness within everything external; for he who is coarse or corrupt doesn't get any enjoyment from nature, but he who is spiritual gets the greatest pleasure from it.

Then the latter would have the most to lose from death and the former the least, he said.

Of course, I said, just as he for whom a thousand mornings are devastated by a hailstorm loses more than he who loses just one morning, and yet the latter is the one who is unhappier. But here it is generally a question of loss. Indeed, only those who are left behind speak in this way. They have not become accustomed to looking into that world; a bit as if someone were released from his plough or his herd and given the leadership and he only told his former workmates that he had lost his plough or his herd. It seems to me that we must rather ask what he who has already lived spiritually here gains at death; and I have no doubt that what he gains is the perfection of that very thing toward which he most strove in this life and that therefore must necessarily be something higher than this present life. For doesn't the external hold a far superior power over the internal here, because here it is more perfect by also containing the internal within it, whereas the internal doesn't by any means contain the external within it in the same way? And doesn't it follow that even this externality couldn't yet be the most perfect of all, because it can't reconcile itself with perfect internality; for if it were the most perfect of all, there could no longer be any contradiction at all between it and the internal? [62]

This certainly follows, he said, from what was said before.

Doesn't it also follow, I continued, that here the internal and the external are still in no way alike, but are unlike, not only insofar as that perfect internality doesn't exist at the same time as perfect externality, but also because it doesn't exist within the external itself?

Even this, he said, is necessary, for if they were completely as one within the external, the latter would immediately fuse into the internal and the internal into the external again.

Then isn't even the external still here as a subordinated externality that is related to perfect internality, as the lower is to the higher?

Of course, he said.

And will perfect internality ever be possible within this sphere of life or when the external has attained such predominance?

He denied it.

Not even with the most perfect externality?

Not even with that, he said.

Thus in order to reach the most perfect internality, we must leave this sphere of life?

Necessarily, he said.

And pass over to a higher one?

Certainly, he said.

And, thus, death wouldn't be a mere reversal of the relationship, whereby at death the external would become completely subordinated to the internal and the subsequent condition would simply be the reverse of the present one; rather, death would be this as well, but at the same time it would also be an elevation into a higher potency, into a really different and higher world?

That, he said, was just what I wanted.

And the wise and just person would not unwillingly give up the present condition for that higher one; instead, once the divine had completely reached maturity and could spread its wings after he had carefully raised and cared for it within himself, he would depart with it and leave behind the imperfect [63] earth from which the divine had sprung. According to the fable, the blossoms of that tree in India transformed into delicate and colorful birds that flew away; and the wise and just person would leave behind this earth with no more feeling than those birds did.

This is beautiful, he said.

But I answered: We are still not in the clear yet; for although the present life is a lower one, you ascribed to it the advantage that it nevertheless embraces at the same time the germ of a higher one within it, and thus, to a certain extent, the present life contains more than this latter one does. Or wasn't this how it was?

It certainly was like that, he answered.

But if it is fully grown now it doesn't need the germ as such any more, I said, and in this case its disappearance is no loss. However, I don't know whether it wouldn't be possible to give another response to this.

You should give us this one, too, he said.

Not now, I said, for I noticed that our friend had been lost in her own thoughts for some time now and seemed to be only half listening to our conversation, if at all.

As we became silent, she suddenly came to herself and said, as if we were still at an earlier point in the discussion: I have thought all this afresh and I think it would be desirable to know how the departed one felt in himself; and it seems to me that this would be the best answer to that question (presumably the question about the merits of the future life).

We both agreed.

Then she said: But how is it that death is so generally imagined as a last sleep? Shouldn't it much rather be an awakening?

Perhaps, I said.

And yet, she said, thinking of the deceased as having their last sleep and as resting from their work is such a sweet thought.

Of course, I said. [64]

And I don't know, she continued, but the day's splendor and magnificence seem so external to me, and only when they disappear does what is truly internal emerge; but why does it have to be night?

The night shows, I answered, that what is truly internal within us is still unfulfilled and that for us this belongs to the future and to what is hidden.

If a light were to dawn within night itself, she continued, so that a nightlike day and a daylike night embraced us all, then all our wishes would find their final resting place. Is that why, she added, a moonlit night touches our inner being in such a wonderfully sweet way and, with its intimations of a nearby spirit life, makes a shudder run through our breast?

Certainly, I said. I remember the words of a man who was often not given the recognition he deserved; more than once he said to me: only he who could do while awake what he has to do while asleep would be the perfect philosopher.[4] However, I always said "would be he who was perfectly blessed." And I also firmly believe that such a fate befalls the blessed among our departed and that they are thus described as those having their last sleep, rather than as those who have fallen asleep; and thus, as it were, they are described as those who have escaped sleep from within sleep and as those who have thereby penetrated through to a waking state. But they are described as those having their last sleep, rather than as those who are waking, for even here sleeping is closer to the internal life than waking is.

A famous minister, whom we all know and whom we cannot deny has a gift for observation, Clara said, often recounts how, at the moment of falling into one's final slumber, an indescribable joy flows from one's entire being, and here the soul is in its finest moral and spiritual activity at the same time. Then all one's mistakes pass before one in a most humiliating way and, by contrast, the purer one's heart is, the more blessed this mid condition between waking and sleeping is. This condition is so infinitely different from anything that we call a dream that its clarity surpasses even the most vivid waking thoughts, and any normal mode of existing seems to be only a dream, a slumbering, or a death by comparison.[5] This condition is then transposed into a completely different point of view, into [65] a kind of watching without pictures, wherein everything is nevertheless differentiated in detail and is completely without confusion. This condition, however, usually (as the minister says he knows from various signs, regardless of whether or not it appears to be so short to the person himself) lasts only a second; it disappears in a sudden, shuddering movement and leaves behind in his soul the painful longing for his survival. Soon after that, complete sleep [das gänzliche Einschlafen] follows.

That shuddering movement, the doctor said, is certainly generally recognized as a sign of waking sleep [als Zeichen des wachen Einschlafens].

Shouldn't just this movement be the stroke, I said, through which nature extinguishes the internal light or vision that wants to rise up, and which nature transforms into mere sleep instead?

At least, he answered, there is no greater proof of the superior strength of external nature over our present life than in its transformation of our innermost condition into sleep.

But, I continued, so many credible men and doctors in particular assure us that through the influence of other people, human beings, acting as if dead toward everything apart from the influencer, and with their external senses completely deadened, can pass over into an internal clarity of the highest kind and to a consciousness of themselves that bears no distant comparison to that in waking life [im Wachen].⁶ If this is true, then I believe that here we would have the experience of a condition that we could justifiably call a higher one and that we could consider to be a wakeful sleep or a sleeping wakefulness.ⁱᵛ And I would thereby compare it not to death, but to the condition that follows death, and one which I believe will be the highest and which will be a clairvoyance uninterrupted by a waking up [Erwachen].

At any rate, the doctor said, approaching that higher sleep is very similar to approaching death.

This is necessary, I said, for even here a kind of dying must precede the heightened condition. [66]

I've heard a lot about these mysterious [dunkel] phenomena, Clara said, that were nevertheless kept hidden from me even when in my very closest proximity. But how they are from the outside does not interest me; I would rather know what people who sleep in this way actually feel.

If, the doctor answered, one were to conclude something about this merely from their external appearance, then they have an indescribable sense of well-being. All the strains of illness fade from their features, they look happier, more spiritual, often younger. All traces of pain fade away from the gladdened face; at the same time everything becomes more spiritual, especially the voice.

O charitable hand of death! Clara intervened, that's how I recognize you! You remind me of my friend who became transfigured so young, who had been my guardian angel in life, and how all this happened to her. How, as the shadow of death was approaching, a heavenly transfiguration shone within her whole being, and that I believed never to have seen her so beautiful as in that moment approaching her demise and never would I have believed there to be such grace in death; how her voice, which always had a melodic sound, then became heavenly music, spiritual tones, which even now sound more deeply in my inner being than the very first chord of a softly tuned harmonica.⁷

If one asks those who have been put to sleep [jene Entschlafenen] about their condition, the doctor continued, they attest that it is a most spiritual one, that they do not feel their body at all or the pain they previously had, and that a divine clarity, a warm light flows through their inner being.

Yes, even before death, Clara said, the ravages of illness subside, the pain stops, and many, predominantly the best, depart in a heavenly delight.

And yet, the doctor continued, this condition is still merely an approximation to the highest one; they are still affected by external things. Although they have their eyes closed, they see everything that is externally perceptible; indeed, many of their senses seem to be a lot sharper.

So what is that highest condition, then? Clara asked.

---

iv. Note by K. F. A. Schelling: Cf. *Stuttgart Private Lectures*, vol. 7, 47.

When they are completely released from the sensible world [67] and are connected to things that are external to them through the influencer alone, only then are they quite dead to the external world. For although previously they were sensitive to the slightest noise—indeed, to sounds that no other ear could perceive at that distance—they are now wakened neither by the rattle of coaches nor by the firing of cannons, and the only human voice that gets through to them is that of him alone to whom they are connected.

And only then, Clara asked, does the highest clairvoyance come about?

Of course, the doctor said. At just this point the highest, inner life is revealed. Everything heralds their most profound consciousness; it is as if their whole essence were pressed into One focal point that unites past, present, and future within itself. Far from their memory being lost, the past from far back becomes clear to them, as does the future, and often the remote future at that.

Doesn't it follow from all these phenomena, I replied, that the spiritual essence of our corporeality, the essence that follows us in death, was actually already present within us before, and that it's not that the spiritual essence arises only at death, but rather that it simply becomes free and its true character comes forth once the senses and other of life's ties no longer bind it to the external world?

The doctor affirmed this and added: A whole range of phenomena during life, which cannot be derived from either the soul or the body as such, testify to the presence of that essence.

To me the profundity [*Innigkeit*] of consciousness is what I love most about that condition, Clara said. I have never been able to understand how so many people can faintheartedly doubt that consciousness doesn't expire or dissipate after death. For to me death always seemed to be something that assembles rather than disperses, something that promotes depth and not superficiality.

That doubt-ridden way of speaking is nevertheless explicable, I said, because for most people death was, and still is, a complete separation from everything physical and this (the physical) seems to me to be at least the basis for any awareness at all.

How? Clara asked. [68]

My dear, I said, with the survival of consciousness [*Bewusstsein*] you are thinking first and foremost about the surviving unity of what is actively conscious [*des Bewusstseienden*], are you not?

Without a doubt, she said.

And, as that which always remains the same, what is actively conscious differs from everything else?

Certainly.

Now "this" and "that," which are required for differentiation, can't be found anywhere apart from within the physical?—Or, I said after a while, because this doesn't seem clear enough to you, if you consider yourself *as* yourself and thus as a person differentiated from everything else, don't you then feel that something lies at the very basis of your consciousness that no concept can unravel, something dark and obscure, something that acts as it were as a support for your personality?

I certainly feel the dark obscurity, Clara said, but it is just this obscurity that I wish would go—it disturbs the purity of the essence.

My dear, once aroused it cannot be made to go away, I said, and nor should it go, either, for with it personality, too, would disappear. But it can become transformed, it can itself become clear and light, that is, as the mute vessel of the higher light, keeping individuality for this alone rather than for itself, and to let the light have a root and a base.

As the diamond is, as it were, only there for the light, she asked, so that the light can shine and reflect through it and it can be something in which the light can grasp itself?

Just like that, I said.

Shall we now say, I continued, that what is in itself dark and obscure comes from *nature* or from elsewhere?

From nature, without a doubt.

Shall we say that from the very beginning each person carries that obscure germ within them or, perhaps, that it is a quite chance growth?

It would be impossible to think the latter, she said.

And shall we say that although this germ is capable of a continual transformation, it [69] isn't capable of destruction, or shall we say that it can be as transforming as it can be destructive?

We must necessarily suppose the first alternative, she said.

But the germ has something physical about it? I continued to ask.

Of course, she said, if it comes to us from nature.

So, then, something physical must also follow us in death?

Necessarily so, if that germ does follow us—

And also, I added, if consciousness of our self remains as our self?

She agreed with this, too.

Now, I said, shouldn't just that spiritual essence of our corporeality be the germ that follows us?

So it seems, she said.

The germ that has itself developed from corporeality into spirituality?

Of course, she said.

But that always keeps its relationship to the physical?

Certainly, she answered, for it is still the essence of corporeality, nevertheless.

And it can never lose the relation it had to that from which it was taken originally?

Never, it appears.

Now, isn't it quite natural, I continued, for those who admit that the spiritual may often influence the physical not to understand that the physical similarly impinges on the spirit world, too? Isn't it natural, I say, for them to be frightened if they think that death separates and completely annuls the link between soul and body, if they think that even individual consciousness may then dissolve and melt away like the fragrance of a decaying flower disappearing into the air, without a single trace of it remaining?

It is quite natural, she said.

But even in this life, I continued, a very few successfully transform that dark and obscure germ within them into clarity and light. For it seems to me, at least, that the masses are almost purely comprised of people [70] who defiantly insist on their individuality and who think that asserting oneself and having an impact comes before all else.

Of course, she said.

And they think and judge accordingly, too, directing all their mental and spiritual activity to this end; so that, for example, they are incapable of forgetting their self as they think, or of becoming lost in the contemplation of the eternal and divine. Instead, they constantly desire something external, something that they can put in front of them and handle as they please; they even completely reject the divine when they notice that it cannot be handled like this. Now, then, if those who seem to be conscious only of themselves should have an experience out of or apart from their self [ein Aussersich haben], will they be capable of that highest consciousness, or will they not far more likely be the sworn enemy of all clairvoyance?

Probably the latter, she said.

Thus, when it is said that after death the best pass on to that very condition that is that most highly profound consciousness, mustn't people believe, and also try to make others believe, that at death all personal consciousness disappears?

It seems that they must say that, she said.

But how then, I said, can there still be something within us that differentiates us from God if that initial dark and obscure germ within us has been wholly transformed into clarity and light?

I don't quite understand the question, she said.

It is also very vague, I said. Let's try it from this point of view, then. You agree that all things or at least we humans are in God?

Even this isn't clear, she said, and can be taken in more than one way.

Very well, then, I said, it is generally said of the blessed, at least, that they go to God, that they are before God, and even that they rest in God. Or should we consider all this as just a beautiful figure of speech that doesn't correspond to anything in reality? [71]

Certainly not, she said.

But that they go to God when they die, it is said, illustrates that they were not with Him beforehand but were separated from Him; it illustrates that they were not in their true homeland but in a land that was foreign to them.

Of course, she said.

But, nevertheless, in respect of what truly actively is [das wahrhaft Seiende], of that perfection within them, they could not be separated from God?

So it is generally assumed, she said.

So, they can be separated from God only in respect of what wrongly actively is [das falsch Seiende] within them?

So it appears, she said.

So, then, I continued, God was within what was perfect in them but, on the other hand, with their imperfection they were not within God?

That is evident, she said.

But the imperfection shall certainly perish, or if not that, it shall be transformed into perfection. It shall certainly remain what actively is, but only insofar as this is necessary for it to make its own beingness the vessel for the higher.

Of course.

And this transformation begins even here, at least for good people.

Always.

But the more they progress toward perfection, the less they are necessarily separated from God.

Of course, she said.

So that as they become more and more perfect, they eventually pass over into God completely, and finally they even disappear within Him.

That seems to follow quite naturally, she said.

But, I said, don't many people generally fear that once they have become completely transfigured their self-will will be completely overcome and they might then disintegrate entirely? Don't they fear that they will no longer actually be anywhere, but will become indistinct within God? And, again, aren't there others who imagine it correctly and with love [72]; that is, they imagine how the soul disappears in God like a drop in the ocean or a ray of light in the sun?

I, too, have certainly read about people like that, she said.

And yet there is something necessary about that idea, I continued, for absolutely everyone—including us—says that blessedness is possible only when there is a perfect unity with God.

Of course, she answered.

Only I don't quite see, I continued, that it necessarily follows that we would lose our particular existence if we became completely one with the Divine. For the drop in the ocean nevertheless always is this drop, even if it isn't distinguished as such. So, too, the single spark from the fire or the single ray of the sun (if there is such a thing) always is that spark or that single ray, even if they aren't seen as particulars. Thus, if we also imagine that at death the pious would be enraptured by God in a blessed delight as if by a universal magnet to which everything is attracted, such that they would now be completely suffused by Him and would see, feel, and want only within Him, then I don't see why their whole individuality would thereby be lost at the same time. In death do they stand in the same relationship to God as those in a magnetic sleep do to their doctor or savior? That is, would they be dead to everything apart from him to whom, conversely, they would be alive and receptive to the greatest degree, and would they experience everything else within Him and have no will other than His own? If so, I would like to know whether all individual existence would be completely lost or, rather, whether individual existence would be raised to its greatest profundity? And doesn't it seem that those who make out that they fear the destruction of their individuality in that perfect unity with the Divine are actually afraid only of that rapture and complete surrender, just as even here they are afraid of all drunkenness—even spiritual drunkenness—and regard him who is replete with the highest things as a madman [73], and consider the death of their own will as actual death or as something even more terrible?

It seems to me, she said in response, there is something we still haven't touched upon here.

Perhaps, I answered. What is it, then?

Just this, she said, that, in the example above, although each little speck of dust in all those that rush toward the magnet and into this link is certainly completely suffused by the magnet's strength and wouldn't like to get out of the invigorating chain, even if it could (as long as it appears to it that it is in it), each speck nevertheless still has something in it that it does not have from the magnet. It is the same with the person in magnetic sleep in the other example.

Excellent, I said, and quite to the point, as they say! So, do they believe that if man has already striven towards morality in this life, this is the only thing that he takes with him and is that through which he can unite himself completely with the Divine in that other life?

They must indeed believe this, she said.

So, I said, nothing physical follows him there?

Nothing; so it seems.

Not even that initial dark and obscure germ, which only gradually receives clarity and light into itself through a kind of divine transformation?

Not even this.

And which nevertheless never denies its primal nature when completely transformed?[v]

It seems to me that this is as unlikely as the clearest diamond thereby ceasing to be hard or material, she said.

But even when this dark and obscure speck of our existence, I continued, is completely liberated and transfigured, it nevertheless always leaves something behind in us *that was not from God*. [74]

From what, then? Clara asked.

Haven't you yourself said that it comes only from nature?

Of course, she said. But those who teach that all individuality disappears in God say of nature that it, too, is God.

As the saying goes, I replied, they may well have heard the clock strike but forgotten the number of chimes. That is, perhaps they heard once: God is in nature, and simply forgot that little word *in*, or perhaps they understand it as if nature were God's inner being and then generally say that nature is God.

My dear, she exclaimed, how often have I heard you say yourself that everything belongs to God and that nothing is outside of God?

---

v. Marginal note by F. W. J. Schelling: Always remains what actively is excited.

Of course, I said, just as a lot belongs to us that is not thereby *we ourselves*; there are also some things in us, if we speak about "us" in a general and broad way, that don't belong to our real self.

I expected her to answer and so I looked at her. But she said: Carry on speaking: a light from a previous time is flickering; a discussion that I'd almost forgotten is starting to come back.

So I continued and said: That's just what that spiritual essence is like that develops from our corporeality and is the seat of presentiment, an organ of what is forthcoming, our trusty companion in this life following us into the future one; but woe to him who considers what lives only in the spirit to be his real self. And so, too, or even more so, with the body, for the seat of desire and passion within us may belong to us but it isn't we ourselves. For don't we in general demand that our real self should rule this other, unreal self?

Of course, she said.

And we differentiate the former from the latter?

Yes, very much so, was her answer.

If, then, nature belongs to God, as indeed it does, then it can't belong to Him as His real and first essence, but only as His unreal and other essence, as something that in relation to His [75] inner essence—what actually actively is—is what actively is not. And yet earlier, I continued, we differentiated between the internal and the external. Didn't we say that the internal is what actually actively is in the external, but that the external was its mere beingness?

I remember, she said.

So, can't we say that within nature God is what actively is, but that nature is only the beingness of God?

Of course.

Only that this beingness of God is, in turn, itself in every way a very living thing, just as artists also still embellish the soles of Jupiter's Olympian feet with life.[8] And if we speak in this way, we are by no means saying that God and nature are one and the same.[9]

By no means, she answered.

Now, if God raises or creates us from this lower part of his essence that is not He Himself, then our initial essence is one whose very basis is different from God?

Of course.

And, just because of that, it can rise through its own activity in order either to transfigure itself into what actively is, in accordance with the spirit, or to oppose itself to it? A bit like how a flower comes up only through the invigorating power of the sun, but nevertheless also comes up through its own effort from a dark base independent of the sun, and finally itself transfigures its innate darkness into light—nevertheless remaining different from the light and sun and still originating from another source and, though becoming reconciled with the light, it is not itself light.

I understand, she said.

Thus, so that even when we are absorbed in spiritual bliss after death, completely suffused by the divine presence and not wishing to leave the blissful world even if we could, something nevertheless remains in us that is differentiated from God and, though lying quietly, it remains there eternally as our first chance either to separate ourselves from Him, as He who actively is, or for us to be within Him independently. [76]

That certainly follows, she said.

And only now, with the complete transfiguration of the innate dark obscurity within us, does the clearest and most profound consciousness of our self and of our whole condition rise up—not only of our present condition but of our past one, too. And far from melting away like ice does in water, it now becomes perfect consciousness, in relation to which our present consciousness is only like twilight or a dream, continually obscured and limited by a conflicting unconsciousness.

She agreed with this, too.

But I was now determined to break up the discussion; the smaller children had already been sleeping over their toys for some time. However, the older girls, who also no longer had anything to do, had come into the inner room one after the other and had cuddled up with Clara. But the doctor had another question ready, which he shot quickly in my direction and which I tried to answer just as quickly, too. Just as conversations about such things are best heard while whiling away the night, and usually end up keeping the company together longer through the shudders they provoke, so, too, here we were suddenly drawn into such a discussion for longer than we'd intended. That is, the doctor said that the only thing he hadn't liked about what had been put forward was the supposition that the condition of clairvoyance was the one that quite generally came after death, when it had been said that this condition in and of itself was a spiritual one: it may be possible for a few to pass over into such a spiritual condition straight after life, but it was completely impossible that everyone should do so.

So I replied quickly and said: I certainly remember saying at least once that it is only the best who experience that; but we haven't examined what happens to the others at all.

However, Clara thought that the conversation would be quite incomplete [77] without this; we were all together for once and, as she put it, I was just in full flow.

But I said to her: Do you believe, then, that it's so easy to talk about this satisfactorily? For it would be easy if I wanted to speak only about the complete opposite of that good condition, the one that awaits those who are wholly and perfectly evil. But just as there are countless intermediate levels between good and bad in this life, so, too, are there between bliss and wretchedness in that life. And that invisible kingdom is not as simple as many think it is; rather, if the saying holds true that each will be done by according to how he thought and acted in his corporeal life, that kingdom must look quite wonderfully diverse. But who would dare to fathom and expound on the wonders of that inner world, when we are still so barred from the wonders of the external world that we see daily with our own eyes. Truly, anyone who dared to speak authoritatively about this would have to have died and come back to this life from the other side, like Plato's Armenian,[10] or must have had his inner being opened to him in some other way so that he could look into that world, as happened to that Swedish visionary.[11]

However, the doctor thought that if one had the two extremes of something, then whatever lay between them could surely be worked out.

I answered: This may not always be the case; and, besides, here it is difficult even to find that other extreme. For just see whether we mustn't go back even further, and whether we haven't already been too quick in asserting so absolutely that death is generally a transference into the spiritual. For there may be so many intermediate stages from a person's present corporeality right up to spirituality that at death he could, indeed, break free from the former without thereby passing over into the spiritual and completely leaving the external, corporeal world. Even he in whom lies the good germ of progression can become spiritual only step by step. But when he who was already ruled here by a retrograde or evil will is in the position [78] where he is forced to advance because of the loss of his body, a keen indignation will rise in him along with a strong yearning for the body. This is particularly so for any spiritual-bodily being accustomed to receiving all its impressions from below or from the body, rather than being subordinated to the soul and being led by the influences of a higher world. Thus, even now this will remain supreme and will continually strive to draw the soul back into corporeality, like a weight hanging on it. And that this is necessarily so is shown by the consistency of the tales coming independently from all nations that such souls frequently appear at gravestones or at places of their choice; now, we can suppose these stories to be true or reject them as completely untrue, as is the fashion today.

At this point a lively discussion broke out about this whole subject, with everyone participating, as always happens when this subject matter is touched upon within a tight-knit circle. In particular, Clara declared that she was completely against all tales of this sort.

They offend all good sense, she said, through their common vulgarity, and they show their origin clearly enough thereby. Rather than arousing belief in these things, which is what you perhaps have in mind, compilations of this kind produce the most definite aversion to them instead; and who can believe in something that he finds common and repulsive?

The doctor, who had already made himself out to be a defender, replied partly in jest by saying that of course the unfortunate did, indeed, represent the very worst of society and were the real scum of mankind, and he replied partly with the remark that all the same there were charming accounts of this kind, too; whereupon he touched upon a few, such as that of Clairon.[12]

But it is just these stories, she said, that I can't make sense of at all. How can I possibly believe that the departed still have so much autocracy that they can affect our environment as they wish, that after death they can even take revenge on such a delicate creature as Clairon? I do not even dare to [79] say whether we should possibly consider such stories to be moral.

But, he replied, if so many natural scientists with all their experience are right when they speak about a spiritual sphere of influence that every living thing has and the kind of freedom that can be effected through it, then shouldn't it also be possible that if this essence is released it could affect the very same essence in things immediately and could thus bring about changes in a completely different way than we do? For to bring about a sound or something of this kind we produce a change in the external world first, by blowing or pushing or by doing something similar, and the internal is thereby moved only indirectly, apart from within our own body, where it is indisputable that the will first stimulates the internal immediately and only then stimulates the external through this. Thus, it doesn't seem impossible to think that when released from its own body that essence could have greater freedom to affect other things and that, like a corrosive, it could free that similar essence within them, too. And perhaps sound, which seems so closely related to those essences anyway, is just what is most easily released in this way, for in some instances sound appears to become released even within nature, not through bodily shock but in a spiritual way. But in general, he continued, that spiritual-corporeal essence is even now the very organ of spontaneity or the medium by dint of which we can in some cases bring about changes merely through will. What is that incomprehensible and yet visible essence that flows from the eyes in the first flush of love or of anger, and where does this bewitching power come from in good and evil that uses just that most spiritual device of all? Where does the undeniably great influence come from of the will itself on the efficacy of the medium, so that it often seems to be merely a medium through which the transmitter's intention operates? What force do the enraptured hold over that spiritual-sensible essence, so that not only can they completely withdraw it from the body—[80] like the priest who was able to shut himself off from all sensory feelings and to be as indifferent as a dead person even to intense pain—but also that the sense of hearing, which is the last to go in death, is moderated to such an extent that although the voices of those who are speaking can be perceived, they are heard as if from a great distance! Even separating that essence from oneself and sending it into the distance doesn't seem to be impossible for those who yearn. How often in French hospitals have I observed the poor Swiss boys who are homesick and whose bodies, though present, are only half alive, if at all; who don't speak and hardly make a sign, their eyes staring fixedly at a single point while their spirit perhaps (so I thought) wandered round their native mountains and cliffs and could have been seen there by someone![13] What I remember having heard or read has also since become very credible to me: namely, that even those in that other life know when a friend or relative will soon be coming because they already see their figure sometime beforehand in the celestial sphere.

I am more prepared to believe in these otherworldly apparitions, Clara responded, than in those on this side, for the soul is surely not where it is, but where it loves, and the truest homesickness is for that other life.

But in any case, I continued after a while, shouldn't the spontaneous use of the spiritual-corporeal essence occur only rarely after death? Aren't there one or more conditions that are midway between clairvoyance and actual sleep? To me, dreams seem to be one such condition and actually an imperfect attempt to effect waking, and hence clairvoyance, within sleep.

Experience, he answered, would at least indicate that sleepwalkers don't dream; on the other hand, as they come out of that state they do start to have dreams, and prophetic ones at that.

So, I said, it would be conceivable that people who almost completely fall prey to external nature at death are seized by a kind of sleep in which they are bombarded by a dreamlike storm of ideas; [81] indeed, even some legends support this. Or is there anything more painful even while alive than to dream of wandering around a gloomy wood or valley and not being able to find the right way, of seeking and not ever being able to find, of being locked in and being unable to get out; things like this often happen to all dreamers. If the imagination is indeed generally the tool through which most people sin, shouldn't the imagination be that through which most people are punished—and shouldn't the tortures that await sinners in the other world consist primarily of tortures of the imagination, whose subject would primarily be the previous corporeal world?

He said that this seemed very probable to him, too.

But, I continued, even if after death the condition of clairvoyance were in general necessary, at least because the departed are connected to the corporeal world only through that spiritual-corporeal essence, a condition opposed to the good one would nevertheless still be conceivable. For haven't you known patients for whom that condition brought feelings of well-being, freedom from pain, and of healing, and yet others who, when brought to that condition, felt intense pain and who sank back much deeper into their affliction?

He affirmed this.

Now, I continued, after death shouldn't it similarly be possible that for those who lived here more inwardly than outwardly the condition of clairvoyance would be a most blessed one through its profundity and freedom from the merely external. But that for those who'd always associated with the body and thus, through this, only with external things, too, and who'd been completely bewitched by the sensuousness of external objects, this condition would bring only torture, for they'd fled this condition here with all their might and had resisted all profundity so as to silence or, had it been possible, even to murder the divine within them and, in a word, had tried to live as externally as possible. For, indeed, here they could bear it partly because, although degenerated, external nature still contains much [82] divine gentleness, which worked as a balsam even on them, and partly because they could completely fill their souls with external things and could, as they so correctly say, thereby distract themselves. But there, where everything external has disappeared and they are left with only the internal condition and no other, they certainly will waver right between beingness and not being. Incapable of having the means by which to enter what actually actively is, and having been cut off through death from what they thought it was—namely, what actively is not—they will try everything to diminish this agony. At times they want to try and rise up, but irresistibly sink back; at times their imagination gets them back into this world again, until they find once more that there is nothing there and that it is a departure from the correct path. These people are fortunate if a higher help, or a call from someone who has passed on, finally brings them onto the right path: and I consider this condition to be one that truly is the purification of the soul that both old and new have spoken about so much. For only a few pass over so pure and free of any love for earthly life that they can be absolved immediately and arrive at the topmost place. But even those in whom an evil will never took root but in whom the original germ of goodness, despite its often being hidden among the thorns of this world and its developments being hindered, never was damaged or completely destroyed—even these people pass over still handicapped by so much vanity, so many false opinions, illusions, and other impurities that they can't possibly immediately join the company of saints, the perfectly blessed, and the found, but must go through many purifications first, some of them having to go through more and others less, each spending a shorter or longer time as appropriate on this path. And certainly such a purification cannot occur without pain. For how can so many corrupt roots be pulled out of a soul, how can so many bends be straightened out, without there being an inexpressible feeling of endless disagreements and objections arising in the area between that evenness and those bends, between the light of God's integrity, which wants to sink into the soul, and the soul's customary [83] constitution, which is completely opposed to this light? Or could everything impure and evil be moved without a deep and painful intervention, be encroached and forced upon by its opposite, killed and thrown from its place? Could all this occur within a soul that had to do with evil and impurity, not just externally but through and through, that was even mixed with it and had grown with it internally, especially a soul that was in the clairvoyant condition or the condition approaching that one, too, which is a much more sensitive condition than the usual one that precedes it? And am I not mistaken, or have I also heard you say that the mere presence of impure people is acutely felt in that condition and in many ways disturbs or even hinders that condition?

Certainly, he said, that's how it is, and he said he knew of many examples.

So, I said, how torturous must the impure person find his own presence, in now being alone with himself and reaping what he has sown, when he passes on to a similar condition after death, or at least to one approaching it. If every evil desire and endeavor can take on a kind of personality, and if every sinful deed carries on living within the person like an evil spirit, how sorely must the soul feel this impure retinue that the soul takes with it into that life! I thus believe that this is most probably settled by the opposing conditions after death. But to speak of only two opposed conditions comes across to me, at least, as very limited; also, it directly follows from the previous reasoning that physically the pure and impure necessarily have to be separated in quite different or even opposed places. But since, even from here, from within the visible, so many stages lead to the invisible, just as body and light are visible but sound is only audible and is invisible (there must be someone who says that it has now been made visible). However, the other two senses in particular—smell and taste—though differentiated in the innermost being of things, can't be manifested through any other medium—and even less so can whatever it is be manifested that has an effect on the varying composition of the air—and yet, [84] according to our external instruments, we would have to conclude the air always remains the same. It is even so with the active agent within illness, which spreads its influence over the whole of the plant and animal kingdom. I say that since all of this is completely invisible and hidden from us, despite being within the visible world, and since each such essence—for example, noise—seems to contain a realm of its own that remains completely for itself alone and that doesn't mix with any other realm, we should take even less exception to the belief that there can be many individual realms and many different kinds of world in the invisible realm we enter after death, each world or realm capable of being the resting place for a single lineage, or for particular lineages. Indeed, we shouldn't take exception to the belief that those many other wonderful places don't lie beyond the vicinity of what is generally called "the visible realm," and that the truth is otherwise than generally believed and which nevertheless appeared so likely; namely, that after death not every soul will be set free immediately and released from this lower area that is Earth, but that perhaps the soul will reach what is actually beyond the senses only through a gradual spiritualization. And it also shouldn't be supposed that everyone stays behind in the lower places for punishment or to be in an intrinsically painful condition. For shouldn't those who lived really moderately and as lawful, brave, and level-headed men, despite living according to the law of external nature, take up some kind of world of peace, an isle of the blessed, so that nothing would be more of a fable than their whole mythology, as the ancients say of the Elysium?[14] For it's difficult to believe that they could pass immediately into the purely spiritual world; yet it's even harder to believe that they stay behind in a painful condition. Rather, it's more fitting that even there each lives according to his belief, so that those who depart while desiring the good and wise God, like Socrates did, or who call God because only a divine Hand can heal them, like Oedipus transfigured at death, will reach their God and will also go there. However, those who had more community with external nature up to that point, without thereby having lived a dastardly or completely god-forsaken life, will perhaps remain in a land of quiet without pain. But they will nevertheless remain in a life that is but a shadow [85] until the drive for a higher existence awakens, as in Achilles's noble soul in Homer, although only as a vain wish to return to this life, when he says: he would prefer to employ a needy man, with neither inheritance nor money, as a daily laborer on the field, than to rule whole groups of the dwindling dead.[15] But what particularly makes me believe in such conditions is not just observing the great majority who live without any enlightenment, or thinking that there really could be a higher life and thus who can relive only this life in another form, as a mere shadow life, but also those obscure words from the forefathers of the Old Testament about a place hidden underground where everything rests, about hell as a power or a resting place that does not let its booty be taken away, even if here and there a ray breaks through lending hope that the righteous won't stay in this place. We cannot pass off all these words as mere fables if we have some respect for the holiness of old transcripts. Yes, isn't it conceivable that the more the spiritual breaks through in this external life, the less the underworld has power over the dead; or shall we consider even those words carried down from Christ about victory over the ancient kingdom of the dead as completely empty, general figures of speech? On the contrary, I believe the following: death really had become a power. As they say, as man went back into external nature and raised the development up into the spiritual, he aggravated and called into reality that terrible force that God had determined to be merely the creature's vessel. The force could not destroy man, but held him fast even in death, apart from those whom God took away. Only when He, through whom in the beginning all things were made, lowered Himself into that sunken and now mortal and transitory nature in order to become, once again, a tie between the spiritual and the natural life even within nature, only then did heaven or the true spirit world become open once more to everyone, and for the second time the bond between earth and heaven was sealed. As He [86] died, the sole light left to man in external nature was extinguished as a sign of the greatest power that death had now exerted. But hardly had he entered into that dark area himself than the earth trembled, the curtain in the temple tore apart—as did the image of this world's separation from the inner sanctuary into which we now have the hope of entering after death—and frequent apparitions of the departed saints signaled to the whole of the sacred city that the power of death had been overcome. And so, my dears, we have come back once more to the sweet festival that we celebrated today and that is the true celebration of the whole of nature's and of man's birth into eternal life. Earth's spiritual age begins from this day, for even Earth must go through it all.

But now, children, let us set off, too, and not stay past midnight, for I already fear that some who may have listened to us would say that we have touched upon thoughts that are excused only by the night. But even if this isn't the case, we should nevertheless stop now.

And so we set off and each of us went home.

IV

At about the same time, a few days or weeks or so later, a philosophy book arrived in which some of the excellent things it contained were written in a completely incomprehensible language and abounded, so to speak, with barbarism.[1] Clara found it on my table and after she'd read it for a while, she said:

Why do today's philosophers find it so impossible to write at least a little in the same way that they speak? Are these terribly artificial words absolutely necessary, can't the same thing be said in a more natural way, and does a book have to be quite unenjoyable for it to be philosophical? I don't mean the obscurity that comes from depth and that only those can see whose eyes are accustomed to looking away from the surface. [87] The deepest, I feel, must also be the clearest; just as what is clearest, e.g., a crystal, by virtue of being such, doesn't seem to get closer to me, but instead seems to withdraw and to become more obscure, and just as I can look into a drop of water as if into an abyss. At any rate, depth must be distinguished from opacity. Depth is one thing, opacity is another. Yet another is the naturally lush growth of a healthy stem on which every branch carries yet new shoots, without the genius intending or particularly noticing them. And another is the intentional mixing of various ingredients to mat them artificially, and which wouldn't leave anything behind other than dead and worthless materials if they were pulled apart again.

I too, I said, prefer to see a philosopher with a sociable garland in his hair than with a scientific crown of thorns, through which he presents himself as the truly tormented *ecce homo* of the people. I am reminded of a saying from Pascal, who said that if one came across excellent thoughts written in an unforced and natural way, one would be charmed and quite beside oneself, for one might have thought to find a special author in such a book; but what one finds is a person.[vi] Depth behaves like what appears to be its opposite, the sublime, in that it has all the greater effect if it is clothed in the simplest words that even working people and craftsmen can understand. The language of the people is as if it were from eternity; the artificial language of the schools is that of yesterday. Anything that is eternal will always try to bring that eternity to expression. And the more gener-

---

vi. Note by K. F. A. Schelling: Pensées diverses 41.

ally that philosophy gains a certain attention, the more astonished I am that this so rarely happens in philosophy, what with philosophy now becoming the representative of revelation for some people and even becoming a great warhead of our time, foreseeing the approaching death in battle, not like Saul swearing his spirit to the prophets and asking about immortality, [88] but like philosophers.[2] Even women come to philosophy lectures now. Doesn't anyone have a female friend, for example, with whom he likes to share his convictions? And if he does, why can't he also speak about higher things to everyone with the same language that he uses with the one he loves?

I remember, Clara said, that when Albert was still with us we would often all have discussions together that would need only to be written down to be generally stimulating. Tell me, why aren't philosophical discussions more generally written?

I answered: Ah, my dear, a lot could be said about that. Philosophical discussions need certain types of people if they are not to be too dull. Certainly, we aren't short of such people: we don't lack enlightened men who are esteemed throughout Germany and who carry the same trust and honor that the Greek Sophists once had, nor do we lack speakers who are contrary and even cheeky and who could put a cunning Socrates to shame; unfortunately the only thing we lack is Socrates himself, a well-recognized and so definite personality. In addition, our philosophers usually debate only lengthy, drawn-out discussions by means of print, which is almost as if two people, one from Europe and the other from America, were playing chess with each other, whereby a dramatic life is hardly possible. For, as they say, writing and printer's ink don't become red; yet, for the sake of whatever reason, some still prize print as a completely splendid and even truly divine invention.

So all the more, she said, should those who understand it erect small stages upon which they could summarize the lengthy debate, pull it into focus, as it were, and make it live before our very eyes.

It would depend on what the attempt was like, I said. If only when we imitated and put across certain personalities they didn't so easily look like an actual person, which wasn't the case with the ancients, and which some people actually tried to do. [89]

Well, then, she said, if we can't take people from the present, why can't we take those from the past?

But not from antiquity, I said, which would make it like some of those tragedies that get ascribed to the Greeks.

No, she answered, from a time closer or more recent to ours. For instance, what splendid philosophical personalities the fifteenth and sixteenth centuries must have to offer, if what they say about the court of the Medicis is true, and what other exemplary personalities must there be from more recent times?

If only it weren't just like that again, I said; that is, with philosophical discourse being more similar to comedy than to tragedy, with it taking more of its material from the present than from the past. If only it weren't otherwise, appearing as cold and arduous despite all its attempts to get at the truth and to give it life. The philosopher who has something correct to say or describe about science won't trouble himself to investigate its remote properties in the way that would be necessary to put it across credibly. For me, at any rate, even strictly observing the dress, speech, and other formalities of earlier times has something about it that goes against the natural freedom of a work of art; how much more so must speech be taken from the present, or must once have been so taken, if it is to have a real effect on us.

Well, then, she said, if the past can't provide the material and yet, with certain reservations, surrounding reality partly can, there is still a middle alternative.

And what's that, then? I asked.

That discussions fitting to our time be devised as if they were taken from the present, but without trying to imitate any particular person; discussions as they could be held now and that, without doubt, really are held. I repeat the question: why can't [90] discussions such as we have between ourselves be written down, whether they be made up or ones that really have taken place?

Oh, my dear, I said, who then would be capable of representing such a Clara as we see before us now, with all the grace and tenderness of speech, all the charm of unexpected idioms, with the inspired spoken play of the gentlest of facial expressions? I, at least, would not be capable of it. And, even then, the discussion shouldn't just stand there as if fallen from heaven, but everyone would naturally demand to know enough about the surroundings and relationships to imagine her as a real person.

Now, she said with a smile, it seems to me that you are capable of doing that, too, and it wouldn't require any extraordinary power of imagination to give a discussion such as ours a historical basis.

And that's just it, I said. How bitterly one would reprimand the person wanting to promote such discussions as having a lack of, or having only a trivial, imagination, just because only a very few reflect that the external must be completely subordinated here and that invention must go to the internal. And, on the contrary, if the historical ingredient sprang only even somewhat to the eye, I can already hear what they will say: see what a cross-breed between novel and philosophical discussion this is; although I already know some novels that are justifiably held in high regard but that, had they been entitled something like morality discussions, would have been shamed not by their content but by their title.

And what would in the end be so bad, she said, about that composition? Doesn't the novel really tend a lot toward dialogue in its life that hovers between the dramatic and the epic? So, it would come back to the question again of whether any form is more natural for our time than that of philosophical discussion.

I don't know, I said, but in its very nature the novel contradicts the unity of time and action; whereas it seems to me that in philosophical discussions this unity is as essential as it is in tragedies, for here everything proceeds so completely internally and everything has to be decided on the spot, as it were, without moving away from the original location because of the narrow [91] context of thought.

Without a doubt, she said with a smile, so that the context of thought resting on delicate, transitory, and often only momentary idioms doesn't fade away?

Of course, I said.

Now, she continued, that seems to me to be the most important objection of all; but it could either be avoided in the way it is actually executed, or the unity that is usually violated could be restored in a higher one.

One must take care, I said, and test it out, for one gets to know the intransigencies of specific forms of art only by practicing them.

Be that as it may, she continued, but I strongly feel the benefit that our time, which mostly desires science so much, could gain by portraying philosophical views in such a way. There are so many complaints about the nonsense put forward by philosophical systems and theories; but doesn't it mainly stem from the artificial language they use?

It is true, I answered, artificial words can be repeated even by someone who is otherwise slow-witted, as has always been the case, and they can still put them together in a way that is nevertheless their own, even if it is one that is silly and foolish.

But, she said, whoever is able to represent the matter within a cosy and nonexternally contrived discussion must really hold the matter, penetrate it, and themselves be completely penetrated by it. Especially, she added, I don't think much of a philosopher who can't make their basic view comprehensible to any educated human being; indeed, if necessary, to any intelligent and well-behaved child. And what is this current separation of academics from the people supposed to bring? Truly, I can see the time come when the people, having had to become thereby more and more ignorant about the highest things, will rise up and make those philosophers account for themselves, saying: You should be the salt of your nation; [92] so why don't you salt us? Give us the spirit's baptism of fire again; we feel that we need it and that we have come back far enough.

And so we spoke some more about this relationship, partly then and partly later.[3]

V

Still at a time bordering between winter and spring, a beautiful day was chosen to climb up to the old chapel in the wood.

On the way Clara recounted: the fishermen told her yesterday that the lake was showing signs of spring, the irregular rise and fall of the water was dying down, and even the waterfowl that go away over winter had been seen. I've longed to see the lake all winter, she continued. We spoke so much and so often about the spirit life and then the picture of the lake would always stand before my eyes. The ancients certainly didn't set the seat of the blessed on islands surrounded by a lake for nothing.

This line of thought seems very natural, the doctor said. The river is more a picture of real life [des wirklichen Lebens]: it draws our imagination along with it into unrestricted bounds, as into a distant future. The lake is a picture of the past, of eternal peace, and of isolation [Abgeschlossenheit].[1]

I confess, she continued, that your talks nevertheless still left me with an unsatisfied wish.

And what is that? I asked.

Should I say? she answered. You spoke so often about places and areas in the invisible realm, and also about places midway between our visible world and the one that is truly invisible; but then you also spoke about a place that was the highest of all, to which only a very few go immediately after death. Now, at the very least, we would so much like to get some idea about this place, the true and actual heaven; or where else should the passion come from that seems to be able to open up to us to some extent and with which everything, albeit still having so very much the appearance of illusion, is received? [93] And even your calling that abode a "place" is very puzzling. Can spirits, too, be in a place?

Indeed, I said, this is one of the most puzzling things of all, for it's based on the mysteriousness of place and space in general, and now I just can't refrain from really putting down some of the foundations. Consider the matter in this way: that since, like all created beings, we can't be eternally for ourselves, we must therefore be conceived within another that embraces all the other beings, too. And now, let's call this the place, just as so many others have also said that God Himself is the spirits' heaven and place, or that His magnificence is.

At least, she said, after your speeches the idea that some people have of looking for their future abode or even heaven in one of the countless stars up above, comes across to me as an almost childish impression.[2]

And yet, I said, wouldn't greater certainty about the starry world beyond our Earth also help us more than a little in these higher questions, for, even here, surely our thoughts can rise up to the invisible only from the visible; and how can we hope to determine anything about the spirit world if we don't yet know what the limits of the visible one are?

It isn't clear to me that this conclusion holds, the doctor said; for although it's important for us to know the limits of things that merge into each other, for things that are complete opposites it seems to be of no account.

But, I answered, I've often doubted just this, and at this very moment I doubt yet again that nature and the spirit world really are as opposed as their concepts would lead us to believe. For, first and foremost, the spirit world is at least just as real a world as this visible one here is; or should we consider the spirit world to be one that exists only in our heads?

By no means, he answered.

Certainly, most people usually consider the spiritual to be less real than the corporeal, I said. And, yet, even this [94] subordinated nature, whose witnesses and observers we are, exhibits so much that is spiritual and that is itself no less real and physical than anything to which we usually so refer. And we have even stated that after death the spiritual is followed by something physical.

Certainly, he said.

So, I continued, mustn't that other, or spiritual, world be in its own way just as physical as this present physical world is in its own way also spiritual?

Clara appeared to be very pleased with this speech and asked me why I hadn't spoken like that in the very first discussion.

I'm just pleased, I said, that now it seems to be giving you twice as much pleasure, yet it was already there underlying our previous thoughts.

With great animation she now requested that I should say what I supposed was physical within that other world.

I said: I will try to turn my mind's eye to the invisible heaven as soon as you or any other friend has relieved me of my ignorance about this visible one.

Nevertheless, she said, that ignorance does not seem to be so great; for no other science is so generally prized for its certainty and import by experts and nonexperts as astronomy is.

Perhaps, I said, the blame lies with me rather than with this science. Unfortunately, like the artist my approval is led by a certain prototype in my head. If something fits with it, I approve of it, even if externally it should seem quite incredible. But if it is rejected by that prototype, then, however externally credible, or, as they say, strongly proven it may be, I cannot believe it. And for me it is just like that, too, with that science. For what those who teach about the stars say they have discovered about the structure of the world as a whole doesn't have the slightest internal probability for me, and what I would find internally probable no one has yet discovered.

So, Clara said, you should let us know what you find probable in accordance with your own feeling and what you find improbable in what's generally been assumed. [95]

We are among ourselves here, I said, and so I could indeed try, but not now, not until we are up there.

We had just come to the point from which the whole lake could be seen for the first time. It was a charming view. The air was still; reflected in the lake was the blue sky hanging over it unmoving and with a few delicate little clouds. Moved only by its own strength, the water lapped at the shore in gentle waves; a flock of birds soared to and fro over the surface and seemed to take pleasure in their own image—some seemed to want to seize it and made themselves wet from head to wing. A delicate promise of green covered the island like a carpet, individual bushes on the graves and in the center were covered with foliage. New grass was coming through on the hills and in the valleys; even the younger trees were hanging with plentiful green buds; only the old, powerful trees, the oaks, beeches, and others, still held their distance from spring, and in front of and behind us, still in their stark, winter form, they stood out from the others. We delighted for a long time in the beautiful view of this area that was coming back to life and then we slowly moved across the glade and up to the old chapel, where we didn't stay long because it was still quite cold and damp. We then climbed right up to the edge of the wood and settled down in the foliage, Clara on the ground opposite the area and we to the sides, and the children diverting themselves round about with the intention of finding violets. As we had now rested and the doctor suggested again that I should express what I had to say, I said:

So then, I will start with a confession or story about myself. Namely, in my early youth I had the habit of understanding everything quite literally. I believed, therefore, that if people spoke about the sun and other self-illuminating stars as being above us, then these stars really were in a higher and much more splendid place than our earth. It was the same if they said of God that he was in the highest or that the souls of the pious were with God in heaven; then I took this quite by the letter, too. Afterwards, as I grew up, [96] I was told better. I was told that "above" and "below" were merely relational concepts and that it was far more correct to say that the sun is below us rather than above us, as, in fact, we are falling and continually pulled toward it, just as we are toward the Earth. But of the other stars, at least, it could just as well be said that they were below us as above us. There was nothing anywhere other than an immeasurable depth and, fundamentally, nothing more than a mere underneath. But a heaven as a higher and more excellent place was no longer there at all; rather, there were nothing but worlds, each of which had its own underneath again in a sun similar to our ours, and even these suns were probably drawn to a yet bigger body. And so it went on deeper and deeper into a quite immeasurable abyss, but always downward; whereby I, for my part, became quite dizzy, particularly in relation to the tremendous figures and the incredible masses. Certainly, I had now understood (for it's not difficult to understand) that the everyday concepts of "above" and "below" are determined by the direction of gravity, but despite this I still couldn't believing in a true above and below. I was once audience to an argument between two people, one of whom maintained that the world extends endlessly into space, the other that it stopped at some point; however, in the opinion of those listening, the former had complete victory and the other went away with me, ashamed and dejected. On the way I tried to console him by saying that he couldn't help but lose against that claim: for once one assumes that the universe is completely indifferent to any direction or to any distance, as they both had done, then there was no longer any reason to stop at anything; it really was more sensible to say that the universe goes right into infinity. If plants didn't turn into flowers and weren't externally constricted, which, however, isn't conceivable in this universe, they would grow on into infinity. Anything that lives can only become complete through a meaningful end point; and so I'd claim that a person's head is what is topmost for him, even if he didn't walk upright, and everywhere [97] I'd generally assume a true above and below, a true right and left, as well as a behind and an ahead. What is completed is generally more excellent and magnificent than infinity; in art it is even the seal of perfection. However, the universe is the most excellent of all, not only in itself but also as the work of a divine artist, and I asked him if he wouldn't have done better to have tackled the matter from this side than with general concepts, and whether he shouldn't have asked his opponent which was the most perfect, an infinite row of worlds, an eternal circle of beings without a final goal of perfection, or a universe that amounted to something definite or perfect. That was then very clear to him, and he set it out yet further in his own way by saying that one can't say of a complete whole that it leaves space beyond it; for as a pillar, for example, has its own space within itself and one can't ask about what's beyond it (if anything is there at all), so, too, does the universe as a work of art encapsulating everything itself have one space only within it; one simply can't ask about what lies beyond it. However, I now became completely strengthened in my belief: I assumed a true above and below once more, and first of all I endeavored to remove the deadly uniformity that erudition had brought into the world. Above all, I doubted whether the earth's gravity, that was so boldly presumed to extend over the whole structure of the world, was effective beyond a certain radius. Certainly, it always seemed to me that the strength from which gravity originated was general, divine, and eternal, but that gravity's relationship to earthly bodies was neither general nor necessary, and that drawing a conclusion from our earth and applying it to the suns was without example and not permitted in any other matter. Thus, instead of a single relationship of gravity to which the suns and then the suns of the suns were supposed to be subordinated, I thought of a great manifold of different ones. And I was more than a little happy when observations found double stars moving alternately round each other but not round a third one, figures [98] of star-wholes that couldn't tolerate the existence of a middle point, such as wholes spread out like fans and masses of light flowing into each other. For, because I found it impossible that inner or spiritual nature had all along been as separate from external nature as it now appears to us to be, I assumed that everything had become like this through the separation and distribution of powers from a divine chaos. Thus, if on one side of the universe the ruggedness of the corporeal has increased and necessarily finally reached its extremity, then on the other side the purely demonic or spiritual must have become predominant, and even in this direction an extremity must have been reached from which a transition into the purely spiritual takes place. Only thus is the universe really complete in both directions. However, if it is additionally supposed, and there are many reasons for so doing, that it wasn't until a later corruption occurred that a part of the universe became completely separated from spiritual nature, then if this part of the universe is not to sink completely and if it is to be used as material for a higher purpose at the same time, it is only all the more necessary to suppose that what is still living and spiritual should be set against what is now dead through a new process of separation, and so a new path of development should be introduced through which divine fruits can still be produced even from the ruined element. Thus, for the very reason that in one part of the universe the power of the external has the upper hand and has completely repressed the internal, the other part remains that much more free, pure, and unadulterated; so that they have now become two worlds when, according to the original divine determination, there should be only one, and now we can pass over into this other, purer world only through death. So, I called this place of purity, simplicity, and health "heaven" and I was no longer afraid not to believe in a heaven that was like an empty space extending indifferently on all sides, but rather to believe in one that was a place up above, according to its nature and formation. And I considered our Earth by comparison to be a part of the lowest area in which, just as Socrates said, we live as if we were at the [99] bottom of the sea, where everything is eaten and eroded by the wet and salt and where nothing, or at least very little, is pure and unspoiled. However, of heaven I supposed that just as nature, in the grips of externality, is unable freely to emerge beyond a certain space or to be penetrated by other things or itself to penetrate them, heaven, by contrast, would have to be what penetrates everything and what is by its very nature all-present. And because both heaven and Earth retain the memory of their original unity and of how fundamentally they belong together, each seeks the other; however, heaven in particular strives as much as possible to draw whatever resembles it from the Earth and calls to the purified souls from Earth to it at their death. Countless are the instances of heavenly effects on Earth, so that, in fact, even now all of earthly life's strength and beauty comes about only through heaven. And so, in spite of its opposition to the visible, I came to think of that spiritual world as only the other side, and to suppose that originally they nevertheless both belonged together and, thus, they were not as separate as most people cared to think. In particular, heaven's perfect worldliness had become clear to me. Namely, that it was just as manifold a whole as this visible world is, if not even more manifold. It was a universe of an immeasurable wealth of objects and relationships and where many places and houses were to be found. Indeed, I even supposed a certain similarity of the two worlds as regards their basic material. For everything that is powerless, suffering, and corporeal in the visible world must be present as active, strong, and spiritual in the invisible one. I also came to the following conclusion: What do we find delightful even in what is most sensuous? Isn't it the spiritual? For what is inactive and corporeal must indeed be quite ineffectual in relation to the higher organs of perception. Doesn't what our senses' fine discriminatory ability discovers in things influence us as a fleeting, incomprehensible essence? Can there be a more spiritual delight than that into which music transports us? [100] In everything it is what is most delicate that is divine. If, then, the divine and spiritual really are native to and at home in that world, then something similar to what moves us here spiritually by means of the senses must be found there, too, and indeed as the finest extract, its root and fragrance, as it were. For there we will consort with the essence of things, instead of first needing to separate the delicate off from its coarse surroundings. There all taste must be good taste, every sound a good sound, language itself must be music, and with one word everything must be in complete harmony; and, in particular, the harmony that surpasses all others and that arises only when two hearts are in accord must be enjoyed more internally and purely. For now it also seemed quite inconceivable to me how I could have doubted that there like was associated with like—namely, what is internally alike—or that any love that was divine and eternal here would find its loved one: not only the loved one that was known here, but also the unknown one for whom a loving soul longed, seeking in vain here the heaven corresponding to what was in their breast; for the law of the heart has no force in this completely external world. Here, related souls are separated by centuries, large distances, or by the intricacies of the world. The worthiest is placed in an unworthy environment like gold in a deposit, crushed in with bad copper or lead. A heart full of nobility and sovereignty finds around it a world that is often savage and degraded and that drags even heavenly purity and beauty down to the level of the mean and ugly. But there, where the external is completely subordinated to the internal, as here the internal is to the external, everything must attract whatever is relative to its own inner substance and worth and must stay in an eternal and indissoluble harmony, rather than in one that is destructive or temporary. And sympathy, which is a heavenly appearance even here, only expressed much more dully and weakly, must reach a completely new degree of profundity there—just as we notice here that bodies transported into a more spiritual condition sense their relationships to each other more profoundly, or that often, as I have been told [101], a touching sympathy sets in between people whose doctor brought them to clairvoyance, and what one feels the other also feels as if he were experiencing it himself, and desire and pain become shared equally. And I don't doubt concerning the expression of this sympathy that it's far more perfect than what's possible here. For even language contains a spiritual essence and a corporeal element. But, like everything, the corporeal is limited and is as if dead compared to the spiritual; they are also dissimilar in every way and mutually impenetrable. There are wonderful cases where even bodies appear to lose this characteristic in relation to each other: thus, certain strange cases that cannot be gainsaid are told of people in conditions of rapture coming to understand languages of which they had no prior knowledge, even of their coming to speak in other tongues, as the apostles once did.³ It would follow from this that in all languages, particularly in the original ones, something of the initial element's purity is still to be found. However, it must be the true common language that is spoken in the spirit world, where only the fully released and free corporeality follows us and where only those words can be heard that are one with the essentials or archetypes of things. For each thing carries within itself a living word, as a tie between vowel and consonant, that is that thing's heart and its inner being. There, however, language won't be requisite for communication as it is here, nor will it be a means of hiding rather than revealing its inner being; but, as here, there is—in a very limited way—communication without signs via an invisible, but perhaps nevertheless physical, influence. So, too, this kind of communication will be quite perfect there and applied with the greatest freedom. So, I don't doubt that there the divine youth who, while painting the transfiguration of the master, himself departed transfigured, will require neither stone, wood, nor paints for his depiction, but will immediately bring the idea of the archetypes to life, of which here he could show only the images. And so, still many other magnificent things could be predicted about that place [102], not by just making it up as takes our fancy, but by following through firmly grounded concepts. Although those living here would find most of them incredible, as is to be concluded from how many mourn for the dead; not only for themselves, in having been left behind by those whom they most loved of all in life, but also for the sake of the deceased person, too, as if they too were now robbed of many friends they could have enjoyed here. However, I will never be able to persuade myself either that any excellent thing that even the present, subordinated life offers us to enjoy won't be found there much more magnificently and purely, or that—far from the future life's being the better one for good people—the future life should rather be a lower and worse one. If, on the other hand, it's true that something spiritual lies at the basis of all sensible existence and that what is actually excellent is within the spiritual, this must necessarily remain so, such that I can't even consider death to be, as they say, a mortal leap and, truth be said, nor can I even consider it to be a simple transition into the spiritual condition, but only one into a much more spiritual one.

During this speech we'd noticed a woman below, walking around under the trees by the church, who seemed to be looking for the offertory box, into which we afterwards saw her throw something. She was now coming toward us, but, as she came into our view halfway up, she stood still and appeared undecided as to whether she should turn back around. However, she composed herself and came up; I recognized her as the wife of a grocer from a small town three hours away from here. As she greeted us, I asked her what had brought her here; but she didn't want to say until I told her that I'd noticed her making an offering down there and that she must therefore have some matter of concern. Oh, no, she answered, I'll admit it just to you, I know you're a mild-mannered gentleman and that you won't hurt my feelings. Last new year my youngest child, a boy and the one whom my husband loved the most of all his children, fell into a high fever that became more and more dangerous. The father was just away at a trade fair and I was mortally afraid. [103] Oh, I said, what if I should lose his favorite child and just when I'm alone. How shall I receive the father, how shall I meet him with the news: won't he perhaps think that something had been overlooked and grieve twice as much. As I lamented in this way, a neighbor took me to one side and said to me: I want to tell you something in confidence, make a vow to St. Walderich of——, he has heard many vows already and has worked true miracles; and then he told me a lot of stories and told me that once he himself had been helped in this way at a time of need.[4] I told him: Where did he get the idea that a Protestant woman such as myself should make a vow to a Catholic saint? God will help me even without that, if He wants. Nevertheless, this matter stayed in my mind, particularly since he recounted that a lot of Protestant people from the whole area placed their trust in St. Walderich, just as the Catholics did. Because his chapel had stood there from time immemorial and was the first in the area, they didn't let it be taken; and every year a big offering takes place in the church, with even the Protestants conceding to attend; and they even hold a service there a few times in the summer besides. But I always remained steadfast, although the man brought yet other people asking me to do it, and one even said: Don't miss this opportunity; you're taking a great responsibility on yourself; if your husband were here he'd certainly do it—which struck me right to the core. Finally, the terrible evening came when the doctor told me this was the last time he'd be there and that I should be prepared for the child to die that night. I was now completely desolate; and as the child was getting visibly worse and worse and there seemed to be no more help at all, I was overcome and inwardly I made a heartfelt, profound vow of a great offering to St. Walderich if he would help me in my need. And you see, she continued, hardly half an hour had passed when the child fell into a gentle sleep and slept right on through until morning, at which point I let the doctor know. He came and was completely astonished that the child was still alive, examined the child when he woke up, and said that the child had been saved; but it's [104] truly a miracle, he said, not knowing about my vow. A few days later my husband came and rejoiced no less than I and immediately gave all of his year's profits and more in order to fulfill what had been promised. So, today I was down there in the small town to collect part of the money from another grocer who still owed my husband, and I'm now going over the hill back home.

I said to her: God has surely helped you, for He sees into the heart. Go home comforted and greet your husband and your children.

The story had touched us all incredibly, so we remained in silence for a while before we set off again. How gratifying it is, I said as we were going away, just to find some kind of belief in these times. For because belief is relevant to everything from the smallest to the greatest, the lack of it makes it necessary that what concerns us retreats further and further back.

But, Clara said, shouldn't it really be assumed that through the magic of belief, through spirits having been shown a certain respect in particular locations for a long time, that they really do become the protective spirits of those areas? Isn't it natural that those who first brought the light of belief into these woods, planted the hills with vines and the valleys with corn, and were thus responsible for there being a more human life in areas that were previously wild and almost inaccessible, isn't it natural, I say, that they also continue to share in the fates of the countries and of the peoples, both of which having been built through them and become united in one belief? Do fathers in heaven forget their children on Earth? And aren't the former the true, spiritual fathers? I, at least, am touched by the sight of a people who still have a protective spirit to which they can turn when in need and from which they can expect comfort and help.

Even a locality hides its own secret, the doctor said. Since human thought began, certain doctrines, particular views of the world [105], and views of things have been native to certain areas, not only to large stretches of land, like the Orient, but to small areas right in among masses of those who think differently. But even that higher organ, which otherwise occurs only as a temporary phenomenon in this life, is more constant in some areas and again not merely in larger kingdoms, such as that so-called other sight in the Scottish Highlands but, as I know from experience, in quite small areas. Weren't even the ancients' oracles tied to certain areas, even to particular places, and shouldn't we draw the general conclusion from this that locality isn't as irrelevant to the higher as is generally supposed?[5] Indeed, don't we feel a certain spiritual presence in every place, which either attracts us to that place or puts us off? The same also applies to individual periods of time.

How astonished we would be if, I said, not being used to considering merely what is externally given, we noticed that the circumstances we considered to be causes were merely means and conditions and that, just when we perhaps least thought that spirits were busy around us, they were leading us to fortune or misfortune, according to which one we followed.

But why does it happen so seldom, Clara said, and why does it seem to be so difficult for a person's inner being to be opened up to him through which he can, indeed, constantly be in a relationship to a higher world?

It is, I said, like other gifts that are shared out according to favor and not to merit and through which God often raises what's lower and held in low esteem. But there is one secret in particular that most people won't grasp: that those who want such a gift will never share in it, and that the first condition for it is composure and a quiet will. I've known some people who, though otherwise spiritual, never let their imagination rest by day or night, and who tried all means, as they said, to link with their departed loved ones through ecstasy; but [106] they were never blessed with that wish. Instead, it seems that throughout time immemorial those who didn't try anything like this, but who were simple and pious, were those who were deemed worthy of receiving openings from another world. In this sense I consider the decree that man should never seek a link to the spirits to be one that is good and just.

Any intense wish is blameworthy and it doesn't seem possible to have that desire without such an intensity, Clara said.

Shouldn't we generally more often observe the same sensitivity to the departed that we believe we owe to the living? Who knows whether they partake more deeply with us than we think; whether the pain we feel so intensely, the excess of tears we weep for them, isn't capable of unsettling them?

At that moment we stepped out from the trees of the church and the whole area lay once more before us in a mild transfiguration.

After a while of quiet contemplation, Clara said: Where does that deep devotion to Earth come from, independent of all enjoyment we call earthly happiness and consisting of a full appreciation of the invalidity of this life? Why, if our heart is indeed numb to everything external, and considers it with pleasure only as a sign and picture of our inner being, why, even if we are firmly convinced that the other world far exceeds the present one in every way, is there nevertheless the sense that it's hard to part from this Earth; and if we don't have a secret horror of this parting for ourselves, then we have it for others?

Let's recognize even in this human trait the wisdom of the hand that placed it in our soul, I said. Even when we scale down our estimation of this life to its appropriate measure, don't we privately have a feeling that tells us we owe this Earth a certain devotion and that this Earth will always remain close to our hearts, not only as a mother, but also insofar as this Earth shares with us one fate and one hope? Or if the Eternal One hadn't denied us the inevitable glimpse into that other life [107], who could bear the time laid down for him here by God and who wouldn't try to depart this life more quickly, where even in life at its best neither security, stability, nor real satisfaction is attained? Where even a moderate joy leaves a sting, and where a heart seldom at peace draws also from life's delights a refined poison, which finally buries us? And, so, I even believe that it is divine intention that also after death, in the inner being of man, a certain sympathy remains for the Earth of which he was a part; that this parting from it will really be felt, for otherwise death would not be death; and that this feeling is truly embedded in the very depths of our being—because doubtlessly God also knows how to make better use of the solidity and coarseness that we leave behind on Earth than philosophers do.

It appears, the doctor said, that lowering Earth to such a moderate level changes some religious conceptions, too.

I don't agree, I answered. Certainly, the Earth is cast out of its central position. Even if there's at least a divine final intention that the internal be represented as much as possible in the external, then both of the end points—the one where the innermost is maintained in its purest form and the one where it's at its most corporeal and externalized—are more or less equally important. And if we may imagine the living, continual creation as a rotation, as it were, in which the corporeal is constantly raised into the spiritual and the spiritual is lowered into the corporeal, until both elements have more or less suffused with each other and become one, then this rotation would have reached its true purpose only when the highest and most spiritual had descended to the most corporeal and when, similarly, the very lowest and coarsest had risen up to the most spiritual and transfigured. Thus, over the course of the times, at just these most extreme limits of the world, where the growth of creation, as it were, goes over into solid mass and corporeality, the appearance of the purest and most spiritual would have become necessary. And conversely, what [108] comes from the lowest and coarsest—man—in accordance with his final destiny must become raised to the highest and most delicate spirituality. For creation cannot rest until the topmost has come once again to the lowest, and it holds even here that the first must become the last and the last the first.

In general I certainly agree with this, he replied. But we can't claim that it's the Earth that is the lowest and most corporeal point of the whole world; and it's even improbable according to everything we know. We could suppose that the planets become freer in their nature and more liberated from the corporeal the further away they are from the sun, or we could simply hold to astronomers' assessments of density, but in neither case does Earth represent an extremity.

My view isn't exactly that the most extreme point falls within just one planet, I answered. But it can't be denied that the bottommost planets are the regions where corporeality most rules. Man alone would convince me of that. Within him, even the most fleeting and delicate essence seems to be tied to such a tough and hard element; and just because of that I would place him very high up on the ladder of being and would understand why he was favored over those creatures that God either created as if from Himself, without taking anything from the other element—the one that was added to our mixture—or at least that have been formed only from the most delicate part of this other material and have been quickly completed.

It seems, Clara said, that man is in this way like a work of art. Here, too, what is delicate or spiritual receives its highest worth only by asserting its nature through mixing with a conflicting, even barbaric, element. The greatest beauty comes about only when gentleness masters strength.

I remember, I said, having heard before about just this from the northern visionary, too, whose speeches on this point gave me the greatest joy. He thought [109] that the Lord wanted to be born on this Earth for the sake of the *Word*, for only here could it have been multiplied materially and written and preserved to the letter. He said we draw similarities too quickly. It is in itself improbable that any other worldly body has such a species of beings with reason, and which is linked so actively and diversely through its doings and dealings, its language and rules, through war and peace, as the human species is. He even maintained that, far removed from the artificial, complicated relationships to which man has been brought through need, a desire for activity, and generally by a drive for company, species in other worlds live only in families. Also, only oral revelations through spirits and angels take place there and, because those revelations aren't bound to as fixed a medium as we are, they easily disappear again and are lost. In general, the inhabitants of the various worlds are to be regarded as different members of one larger person, in which the people of our Earth represent the natural or external sense. This latter is the last, the one where the inner being of life expires and where it rests as if within its communal being. Similarly, the expressed and written Word is the goal and end of all divine revelation; it is where revelation has completely passed over to the external and where the Word truly has become flesh. And one could even add, I think, that language, as we know it, is something special to Earth. Perhaps in other worlds it is far more elementary and more similar to music, arousing transitory sentiments rather than conveying thoughts, and perhaps plummeting the depths of the heart. It would then be fitting for natural philosophers to see whether that certain degree of liveliness was fitting for the Earth even in another relationship, a degree of liveliness in which the living Word bursts forth; not like the most precious metal of all, but like one that, though less noble, shines most, and—like that sense for which the strong and most corporeal organs were necessary and which is at the same time the innermost one, too—so also, conversely, what mostly appears externally to be internal and [110] spiritual, appears internally to be the most external. Yet this seems to lead to such wonderful entanglements of the internal and external that I do not trust myself to develop this speech any further.

But even taking the matter purely externally as generally done, that is, according to numerical relationships, surely it shouldn't be impossible to find the place and location of Earth once and for all, the doctor replied. For I do not know what hunch it is that makes me so firmly convinced that the Earth must stand in a special relation to the planets, quite apart from my belief that the Earth was the stage for the clearest and most perfect divine revelation. But, to me, most of the attempts to date to find a lawful order between the various worlds seem partly not to be scientific enough and partly to come from unnatural and false assumptions.

If one were to return to the old way of counting, which certainly has a lot going for it, and to the sacred number, which has even more, nothing would prevent it from being continually overtaken by further discoveries, which is only to be expected, taking on a self-repeating septenarius, in which Earth takes the middle position from having been the lowest. But be that as it may, it seems to me that the greatest expectations are justified of an essence raised from such deep darkness into such a light so high. One essence approaches the transformations that in the present world are out of the question, even in the greatest events of its internal and external life, an essence that, like God, seems destined to unite the extreme ends of existence in itself.

[175] **SPRING**

[Spring fragment from K. F. A. Schelling's first single edition, 1862. Text in square brackets preceded by / denotes a *different word* in the Schröter edition of the spring fragment. Text in square brackets not preceded by / indicates *additional text* in the Schröter edition. Text in pointed brackets <> is text that is not found at all in the Schröter edition.]¹

O, Spring, time of longing, with what a zest for life you fill the heart! On the one hand, we are drawn to the spirit realm insofar as we feel that true bliss can exist only in that greatest profundity of life; on the other hand, with its thousandfold magic, nature calls heart and senses alike [176] back into the external life. Is it not hard that neither the internal nor the external alone satisfies us and that yet so few are capable of uniting them both within themselves! Yet it is fundamentally only one and the same life in different forms. Why can't these two forms be at the same time, and our fate be a single united life from the very beginning? You say it was man's own fault that they were separated and I must believe you, for I can see no other explanation for it. But won't they ever both be at the same time? Are they separated forever? Won't the time ever come when the internal will be completely embodied in the external, the external fully transfigured into the internal, together representing only one indestructible life? [(where the external will be completely suffused by the internal and the internal fills the soul of the external?) New paragraph] Or won't [/will] everything within extant nature be completed [some day] through three levels? Isn't the first of nature's powers [itself only] responsible merely for the individual, egotistical existence of things and doesn't another counteract it from the very beginning that <strives towards> [effects] the spiritualization, profundity, and unity of its being, [/?] until at the highest level both powers emerge reconciled in one and the same essence, and an organic, continually active life emerges that is open to everything and yet exists for itself? Don't [177] these very same powers, which still emerge as separate and conflicting in inorganic beings, emerge united and in accord in organic ones? And, in a higher sense, isn't it these very same powers that maintain the conflict in our current life; and in this respect aren't we actually standing just at the very first stage of life? Isn't the spiritualizing power victorious in death and won't we thereby be placed at a higher stage or potency? [new paragraph] But doesn't the actually organic level ever come about within the larger course of nature, a level that nature, nevertheless, does attain within the smaller circle of the lower life? Shouldn't [just] those very same three [stages or] potencies that we see here, more or less at the same time and side by side, also [on the whole appear emerging] <emerge> one after the other and shouldn't there be the same sequence of stages in time that we perceive here in space? And what then would come of that threefold unity of soul, body, and spirit;[/,] or what would come of a completion if [as is claimed, here,] in the present life the corporeal [were dominant and] held spirit and soul prisoner, as it were,[/;] if in the condition after death the spirit would be free,[/;] if the soul, however, would never rise to its true essence? For the soul will rule only when the powers that are still currently in conflict here, when spirit and body are completely reconciled[,] when the forms are one and the same undivided [and thus also truly perfectly blessed] life. Bliss [178] is freedom and the rule of the soul. It is impossible for *this* condition to be complete bliss when the soul is subordinated to the spirit and the body is devoured by its opposite. It is impossible to believe that this wholly corporeal nature appeared from nothing just in order forever to return to nothing some day and to believe that only the spiritual life should be everlasting. Corporeality is not imperfection, but when the body is suffused by the soul, then it is perfection in its plenitude. The merely spiritual life doesn't satisfy our heart.[2] There is something in us that desires a more essential reality; our thoughts come to rest only at the final unity; united life must follow separated life;[. O] <o>nly in perfected externality does the soul find its final peace. And as the artist does not find peace in thinking about his work, but only when he has represented it physically, and as anyone fired by an ideal wants to find or reveal it in a physical-visible form, the goal of all longing is likewise the very perfection of corporeality as a reflection and mirror of perfect spirituality.

Roughly so did Clara address us in the first days of spring, when we were on the hill from which she could see the beloved country of her native land. [179] The broad plain was transformed into a sea of blossom and fragrance [/light]; everything floated with a revived desire and delight; it was one of those moments when, gripped by the all-pervading power of life in nature, we seem to enjoy an eternal present in which no pain could touch us.

Don't be surprised about my sudden speech, she continued as we remained in silence for while. We often spoke a lot about things in the hereafter, but I couldn't rest until my thoughts had penetrated the goal of all times. The spring aroused this blossoming of thought and hope in me. It has become profoundly clear to me and has penetrated my heart that we are nature's children; that, according to our first birth, we belong to her and that we can never wholly dissociate ourselves from her, and if she can't become one with God, our own union with Him must either be imperfect or even impossible. Indeed, not only us, the whole of nature yearns in the God from whom she is initially taken. [new paragraph] Indeed, nature is currently submitted to the law of externality and even she, like everything that lives within her, must go through both forms of life [180] one after the other, which, in accordance with her fate, she couldn't immediately unite. Even this firm structure of the world will one day turn into the spiritual.[; b]< B>ut only this external form will disintegrate, the inner power and truth [/essentiality] will persist to become revealed within a new transfiguration. The divine fire that now rests sealed within her will one day gain the upper hand, and [then] everything that was introduced into her merely by [the power of the external] suppressing the [/suppression of the] truly internal will languish; then, returning to her initial condition, she will no longer be the unauthorized essence [/work] that the divine powers detain in themselves as prisoner, as it were, and the spiritual and divine will voluntarily unite with[in] the purified essence once more. [new paragraph] I speak of this as one who suspects but who has no knowledge.

Even here, <I said,> we will [have to] start out from matter's current degraded and imperfect condition in order to understand its enhancement and perfection; in order to understand the characteristics through which matter will one day be one essence with the spiritual, we will have to consider those through which matter currently seems to be opposed to the spiritual and, indeed, is opposed to it <. . .>

[275] # Sketch

1. Reality of the spirit world (of the past)
2. Perfect humanity of spirits
3. Diversity. Its ideas.
   I. Clairvoyance in general
   II. In particular, of what it consists
      (a) Contrast to science; everything is immediate, nothing mediate; perhaps something about the hierarchy of the sciences. Everything in immediate feeling.
      (b) No struggle—the long peace; sin too is gone
      (c) No memory of things as absent. No past.
      (d) Internality of the community from the last part.
   III. Whether the condition of cl[airvoyance] is also applicable to damnation and whether there isn't a condition between bliss and misfortune.
   IV. On the where?

Appendix

GERMAN SINGLE EDITIONS OF CLARA

In Chronological Order
All single editions include a preface by the relevant editor, although K. F. A. Schelling's preface is very short. Schröter's edition also includes an afterword.

Schelling, K. F. A., ed. *Clara: oder Zusammenhang der Natur mit der Geisterwelt.* By F. W. J. Schelling. Stuttgart: Cotta, 1862.

Schelling, K. F. A., ed. *Clara: oder Zusammenhang der Natur mit der Geisterwelt.* By F. W. J. Schelling. 2nd ed. Stuttgart: Cotta, 1865.

Kuhlenbeck, Ludwig, ed. *Clara: oder über den Zusammenhang der Natur mit der Geisterwelt.* By F. W. J. Schelling. Leipzig: Reclam, 1913.

Ehrenberg, Hans, ed. *Clara: Oder über den Zusammenhang der Natur mit der Geisterwelt.* By F. W. J. Schelling. Stuttgart: Frommanns, 1922.

Schröter, Manfred, ed. *Clara: oder über den Zusammenhang der Natur mit der Geisterwelt.* By F. W. J. Schelling. München: Leibniz, 1948.

Dietzfelbinger, Konrad, ed. *Clara: Über den Zusammenhang der Natur mit der Geisterwelt.* By F. W. J. Schelling. Andechs: Dingfelder, 1987.

TRANSLATIONS OF CLARA

Kessler, Elisabeth, trans. *Clara: ou Du lien de la nature au monde des esprits.* By F. W. J. Schelling. Introduction Jean-François Marquet. Mayenne: L'Herne, 1984.

Necchi, P., and Olphalders, trans. *Clara: Ovvero sulla connessione della natura con il mondo degli spiriti.* By F. W. J. Schelling. Italy: Guerini, 1987.

SELECTED WORKS WITH SUBSTANTIAL DISCUSSIONS OF CLARA

In Alphabetical Order
Beckers, Hubert. *Die Unsterblichkeitslehre Schellings im ganzen Zusammenhange ihrer Entwicklung.* Munich: Verlag der k. Akademie, 1865.

Daumer, G. "Schelling über den Reinigungszustand nach dem Tode." *Der Katholik* 1 (1866): 327-34.

Ehrhardt, Walter E. (forthcoming). Schellings Lehre über Fortdauer und künftiges Leben. Einige Bemerkungen zum Schluß der Vorlesung 'Einleitung in die Philosophie.'

Grau, Alexander. "*Clara*: Über Schellings gleichnamiges Fragment." *Zeitschrift für philosophische Forschung* 51 (1997): 590-610.

Hoffmann, F. "Schellings Unsterblichkeitslehre." *Philosophische Schriften* 6 (1879): 457-72.

Horn, Friedemann. "F. W. J. Schellings Lehre von den letzten Dingen." *Zeitschrift für Religions und Geistesgeschichte* 6 (1954).

Horn, Friedemann. *Schelling and Swedenborg: Mysticism and German Idealism.* Trans. George F. Dole. Pennsylvania: Swedenborg Foundation, 1997.

Maesschalck, Marc. "Essai sur l'anthropologie Schellingienne." *Revue Philosophique de Louvain* 85 (1987): 475-98.

Nosari, Sara. *La favola di Clara: paradigma schellingiano e pedagogia della morte.* Milano: Mursia, 1998

Steinkamp, Fiona. "Schelling's *Clara*: Editors' Obscurity." *Journal of English and Germanic Philology* (2002)

Tilliette, Xavier. *Schelling: Une Philosophie en Devenir.* 2 vols. Paris: Libraire philosophique J. Vrin, 1970. See esp. vol. 1, chap. 3.

Vetö, Miklos, ed. *Stuttgarter Privatvorlesungen: version inéd., accompagnée du texte des oeuvres.* Turin: Bottega d'Erasmo. 1973. Intro. contains thoughtful discussion of dating of *Clara*.

Clara first appeared as "On Nature's Connection to the Spirit World" in F. W. J. von Schelling's *Sämmtliche Werke.* Vol. 9. Ed. K. F. A. Schelling. Stuttgart: Cotta, 1856-1861. 1-110.

ENGLISH TRANSLATIONS OF SCHELLING

In Chronological Order of Translation

Schelling, Friedrich Wilhelm Joseph. *The Philosophy of Art: An Oration on the Relation between the Plastic Arts and Nature.* Trans. A. Johnson. London: Chapman, 1845.

——. *Philosophical Inquiries into the Nature of Human Freedom.* Trans. James Gutman. Chicago: Open Court, 1936.

——. *The Ages of the World.* 1815 draft. Trans. and ed. Frederick de Wolfe Bolman, Jr. New York: ColumbiaUP, 1942.

——. "Concerning the Relation of the Plastic Arts to Nature." Trans. Michael Bullock. *The True Voice of Feeling.* Ed. Herbert Read. New York: Pantheon, 1953.

——. *System of Transcendental Idealism* (conclusion). Trans. A. Hofstadter. *Philosophies of Art and Beauty: Selected Readings in Aesthetics from Plato to Heidegger.* Eds. Hofstadter and R. Kuhns. Chicago, 1964. Rpt. in *The Origins of Modern Critical Thought: German Aesthetic and Literary Criticism from Lessing to Hegel.* Ed. David Simpson. Cambridge: CambridgeUP, 1988.

———. *On University Studies.* Trans. E. S. Morgan. Ed. Norbert Guterman. Athens: Ohio UP, 1966.

———. *The Deities of Samothrace.* Trans. Robert Brown. Missuola, MT: Scholars, 1977.

———. *System of Transcendental Idealism.* Trans. Peter Heath. Charlottesville: U of Virginia P, 1978.

———. "On the Possibility of a Form of all Philosophy." Trans. Fritz Marti. *The Unconditional in Human Knowledge: Four Early Essays (1794-1796).* Ed. Fritz Marti. Lewisburg, PA: Bucknell UP, 1980.

———. "Of the I as Principle of Philosophy: or, On the Unconditional in Human Knowledge." Trans. Fritz Marti. *The Unconditional in Human Knowledge: Four Early Essays (1794-1796).* Ed. Fritz Marti. Lewisburg, PA: Bucknell UP, 1980.

———. "Philosophical Letters on Dogmatism and Criticism." Trans. Fritz Marti. *The Unconditional in Human Knowledge: Four Early Essays (1794-1796).* Ed. Fritz Marti. Lewisburg, PA: Bucknell UP, 1980.

———. "New Deduction of Natural Right." Trans. Fritz Marti. *The Unconditional in Human Knowledge: Four Early Essays (1794-1796).* Ed. Fritz Marti. Lewisburg, PA: Bucknell UP, 1980.

———. *Bruno: or, On the Natural and Divine Principle of Things.* Trans. and ed. Michael G. Vater. Albany: State U of New York P, 1984.

———. "Schelling's Aphorisms of 1805." *Idealistic Studies* 14 (1984): 237-58.

———. *Of Human Freedom.* Trans. Patricia Hayden-Roy. *Philosophy of German Idealism.* Ed. Ernst Behler. New York: Continuum, 1987.

———. *The Philosophy of Art.* Trans. and ed. Douglas W. Stott. Minneapolis: U of Minnesota P, 1988.

———. *Ideas for a Philosophy of Nature.* Trans. and eds. Errol Harris and Peter Heath. Cambridge: Cambridge UP, 1988.

———. "On Modern Dramatic Poetry." From *Philosophy of Art.* Trans. E. Rubenstein and David Simpson. *The Origins of Modern Critical Thought: German Aesthetic and Literary Criticism from Lessing to Hegel.* Ed. David Simpson. Cambridge: CambridgeUP, 1988.

———. *On Dante in Relation to Philosophy.* Trans. E. Rubenstein and David Simpson. *The Origins of Modern Critical Thought: German Aesthetic and Literary Criticism from Lessing to Hegel.* Ed. David Simpson. Cambridge: Cambridge UP, 1988.

———. "Treatise Explicatory of the Idealism in the *Science of Knowledge*" (1797). Trans. Thomas Pfau. *Idealism and the Endgame of Theory: Three Essays by F. W. J. Schelling.* Ed. Thomas Pfau. Albany: State U of New York P, 1993.

———."System of Philosophy in General and of the Philosophy of Nature in Particular" (1804). Trans. Thomas Pfau. *Idealism and the Endgame of Theory: Three Essays by F. W. J. Schelling.* Ed. Thomas Pfau. Albany: State U of New York P, 1993.

———. "Stuttgart Seminars" (1810). Trans. Thomas Pfau. *Idealism and the Endgame of Theory: Three Essays by F. W. J. Schelling.* Ed. Thomas Pfau. Albany: State U of New York P, 1993.

———. *On the History of Modern Philosophy.* Trans. Andrew Bowie. Cambridge: Cambridge UP, 1994.

———. "On the Nature of Philosophy as Science." Trans. M. Weigelt. *German Idealist Philosophy*. Ed. Rüdiger Bubner. London: Penguin, 1997.

———. *Ages of the World*. 1813 draft. Trans. Judith Norman. *The Abyss of Freedom: Ages of the World*. Ann Arbor: U of Michigan P, 1997.

———. *Ages of the World*. 1815 draft. Trans. and ed. Jason Wirth. Albany: State U of New York P, 2000.

NOTES

GENERAL INTRODUCTION

1. For English translations of *The Ages of the World*, see Schelling (1942, 1997, 2001).

2. For English translations of *Of Human Freedom*, see Schelling (1936, 1987).

3. For the English translation of *Bruno*, see Schelling (1984).

4. See Pareyson (1977, 666).

5. The "Stuttgart Seminars" are found in English translation in Pfau (1996).

6. See Tilliette's (1981) footnote to the letter from Paulus to Niethammer on 17 November 1803.

7. Bonaventura's *Die Nachtwachen* appeared in 1805. Although many people at the time thought that Schelling had written the novel, an article in *Euphorion* in 1987 by Ruth Haag appeared to show that the journalist E. A. F. Klingemann was the author. This theory had already been proposed in 1973 by J. Schillemeit. The manuscript was never found in Schelling's literary estate, which is what prompted the controversy over the authorship. More details can be found in Gulyga (1989).

8. Just before this book went to press, Ehrhardt's article in *Unser Harz* was brought to my attention (Ehrhardt 2000). Ehrhardt offers the controversial view that Caroline had a brief relationship with Goethe in August 1784 and that Auguste resulted from this affair. Ehrhardt cites a letter from Caroline to her sister Lotte in which Caroline appears to hint at an affair but in which conspicuously she does not mention Goethe's presence in the area at that time. There were rumors that Caroline was favored by Goethe. Karoline Tischbein drew a portrait (now lost) of Auguste giving Auguste lips and ears that could have been inherited from Goethe. Auguste was buried in the German town of Bad Bocklet and there were plans to erect a monument to her there. Thorvaldsen, a famous sculptor who was responsible for the gravestone of Goethe's son, was commissioned to do the work. Caroline designed the monument. Ehrhardt argues that the monument contains symbolism pointing to Goethe as the father of Auguste. He maintains that this was why the original monument was never erected—it would have given too much away. Traditionally, the explanation for the monument not being placed on public display is that a work by Thorvaldsen was too valuable to be exposed to the elements. Indeed, this is what Goethe noted to Schelling. Ehrhardt comments that, unusually, Goethe offered to compose the inscription. Moreover, in 1830, thirty years after Auguste's death, Goethe asked Countess Jenny von Pappenheim not to let Auguste's resting place be forgotten. In 1960 the town of Bad Bocklet finaly procured a cast of

the monument and it is now there on public display and on their internet pages. The original can be seen in the Thorvaldsen museum in Copenhagen.

9. Ehrhardt (forthcoming) argues that this passage shows that *Clara* was written closer to 1803, for whereas Caroline was known for her skill at reading texts aloud, Auguste wanted to be a singer. Indeed, Auguste died with a song on her lips. Thus it is more fitting to say of Auguste that "her voice which always had a melodic sound then became heavenly music."

10. J. B. Spix (1781–1826) was a doctor and a zoologist. He came to Munich in 1811 and Schelling mentions him in a letter to Schubert dated 4 April 1811.

11. Although note that either the dating of the letter is mistaken or Schelling's calculations are wrong. They got married in 1812, not 1814. Using these dates, the couple was married for 42 years.

CLARA/INTRODUCTION

1. This introduction is present only in Kuhlenbeck's (1913) version of *Clara*. K. F. A. Schelling's footnote is in K. F. A. Schelling's original version of *On Nature's Connection to the Spirit World* in Schelling's *Sämmtliche Werke*, but it is not reproduced in Kuhlenbeck. No other German single edition of *Clara* includes the introduction. Vetö (1973) remarks that Horn (1954) dated the introduction at 1806, although Vetö himself suggests that it is more likely to have been written toward the end of 1810 or in the first few weeks of 1811.

I

1. Thus, this scene is taking place on November 2. All Souls' Day rests on the idea that the faithful on earth need to pray for those who have passed over in order to help purify the dead for the sight of the Divine. The tradition was retained by Protestants but was banned in some churches during the Reformation in the sixteenth century. The banning of this festival in the Reformation is presumably what the clergyman is referring to later on in this section.

2. Note that Schelling often uses the countryside symbolically. Here Schelling deliberately describes the river as a *Band*; that is, as a ribbon or a tie. The river is a barely visible ribbon, but can nevertheless sometimes be seen (like the tie [*Band*] from this world to the next).

3. The Thirty Years' War (or series of wars) took place from 1618 to 1648. It was primarily a religious war, although it also had political aspects. It began when the Protestant magnates in Bohemia elected the Calvinist Frederick to the throne instead of the Catholic emperor Ferdinand. The war ended with the Treaty of Westphalia.

4. The priest does not specify here which of the customs he has in mind. One possibility is the mummification of bodies after death and the provision of food and clothing for them in their grave in the belief that the "whole person" survives death. The body had a soul that could return and reinhabit the body and a spirit that could fly to heaven.

5. *Heiß* (literally: hot) here is being contrasted with "cold" words.

6. Schelling is contrasting *groß* (large) with *klein* (small).

7. The first Charterhouse was set up in 1084 by St. Bruno. Bishop Hugo of Grenoble had dreamt that God wanted to have a place in the wilderness of Chartreuse and that seven stars would show him the way. The arrival of Bruno and six companions looking for a place to lead a hermetic life seemed as if it were a message from God. The number of cloisters grew until the fifteenth century. Those in the Carthusian orders held a vow of silence, had only modest meals, wore coarse clothing as penance, and spent much time in their own rooms reading, praying, writing, and doing handiwork. The Thirty Years' War caused many of the cloisters to close. In 1782 Joseph II began to abolish cloisters in general in Austria (which at that time included a portion of what is now Germany). In keeping with the economics of the time, monks and nuns were seen as disruptive to the state because they did not bring anything to society. The cloisters now either had to close or had to perform a social role such as providing schooling, moral education, or nursing facilities. Likewise, the French Revolution resulted in the closure of many French cloisters. In Austria the public was bombarded with propaganda against cloister life, but this lost Joseph II a lot of popular support. He started to take corrective measures and his successor continued these measures, forbidding jokes against the monks in 1802. Nevertheless, the situation didn't substantially improve for the cloisters until the beginning of the twentieth century (Beck 1987; Kovács 1984). Schelling's characterization of the cloisters here may have been influenced by public opinion at the time, both in the sense of seeing the need for the cloisters to serve a social function and in the sense of outrage at the propaganda against the cloisters and at the execution of the nuns and monks in the French cloisters. Ehrhardt (forthcoming) notes that new laws came in on 27 April 1803, leading to debates about the increase in protestant influence. He believes that in this passage Schelling is referring to these events.

II

1. Ehrhardt (forthcoming) notes that Georg Waitz has suggested that Caroline's handwritten notes on "Gedenke an den Tod!" ("Be mindful of death!") were supposed to be entered here. Ehrhardt writes that Caroline's "Gedenke an den Tod!" is full of memories of a meadow and thus it fits very well with the description of the lilies in the meadow and their pale blue of remembrance that follow the "empty place in Schelling's manuscript."

2. *Zeitlos* as an adjective means "timeless."

3. Schelling may be thinking of the landslide in Rossberg, Switzerland, in 1806. It killed 457 people and covered the village of Goldau (Walter 1996). In 1812 Schelling started to jot down natural events of note in his diary, such as an earthquake in Rome (noted 21 March) and snow in Venice in April (noted 10 April). This temporary desire to make a physical record of such events might be related to his thoughts on nature's reflecting or forewarning world events.

4. In *De Re Metallica* (1546) Agricole mentions that miners used rods to discover minerals and buried treasure; dowsing is also mentioned by Paracelsus. Shepard notes that

divining rods later became universally used in the Harz mountains and in Saxony. Schelling, of course, was heavily involved with Ritter's experiments on the dowser Campetti in 1807-1808; he was therefore most likely well acquainted with the historical and contemporary use of dowsing rods for finding treasure.

    5. In this context *Licht* means "clarification," but it can also be translated as "light." Throughout *Clara* there is much play on the contrast and relationship between clarity and light and obscurity and darkness.

III

    1. Literally "the clearest certainty." As becomes obvious later on in the text, Schelling plays on the similarity between Clara's name and *clear* (*klar*). In the same vein there is a close connection between these words and the term *clairvoyance* (literally: clear seeing).

    2. One contemporary of Schelling who held such a theory was the professor of political economics at Marburg, Johann Heinrich Jung (1740-1817). Jung is better known by his pseudonym of Heinrich Stilling (or hence as Jung-Stilling). He held that a luminous body connected the body and soul to the spiritual. Schelling may also be thinking of Hindu beliefs, which hold that there is a physical, subtle, and causal body. The subtle body can leave the physical and then reenter it.

    3. Schelling may be thinking here of Oetinger's famous observation of the balm leaf. After leaving several such leafs to dry out for some time, he cut them into pieces, poured some oil over them, and found that not only did the oil take on the scent or spirit of the leaves, but that the very form of the leaves was restituted in the solution in every detail. The full description can be found in part 2 of Oetinger's *Philosophie der Alten*, and it is cited in full in Benz (1955, 58).

    4. Tilliette (1970, 562) remarks on this passage that Fichte once noted that Condillac wrote two or three pages of his book while asleep and on waking found them to be sublime. Both Fichte and Hegel expressed skepticism about this. Was Schelling thinking of Condillac as the "man who was often not given the recognition he deserved"?

    5. The minister in question is Lavater. In *Aussichten in die Ewigkeit*, in a series of letters discussing the transition from life to death, Lavater (1778, vol. 4, letter 41, 110-111) writes, "This . . . condition seldom lasts more than a second, although countless moral and metaphysical ideas radiate through me with clarity one after the other. . . . I am placed into new points of view from which I can see everything quite differently from usual and yet so incontrovertibly clear, so true and with such conviction and with such a view and feeling of truth and harmony. It is as if I were capable of thinking without pictures or signs . . . everything can be cognized immediately and in their true similarities and relationships . . . every usual way of existing seems to be only a dream, a slumber, a death in comparison" (my translation). In his diaries, Schelling paraphrases a passage from this volume of Lavater's *Aussichten* on 21 January 1810 (Knatz et al. 1994, 45-46). In paraphrasing Lavater, Schelling focuses on premonitions and the overcoming of passion. Given that Schelling was obviously thinking about Lavater's work at this time, the reference to Lavater in this passage in *Clara* lends support to Vetö's (1973) hypothesis that *Clara* was primarily written between February and July 1810.

6. Much of this discussion of death/magnetic sleep is influenced by Gotthilf Heinrich Schubert's (1808) *Ansichten von der Nachtseite der Naturwissenschaft*. Schubert (1780-1860), later to become a professor of natural history, was a good friend of Schelling. In this book Schubert remarks, for example, on the extraordinary sympathy between the magnetizer and the patient, saying that the patient's will becomes one with that of the magnetizer (345); he notes cases of apparent clairvoyance and precognition; and he claims that, when magnetized, the patient's voice became refined and that he or she would describe their condition as the most blessed they had ever experienced (335). If others came into the room, patients would feel fear and pain even if they did not know that the other people were there (349). Moreover, Schubert explicitly suggests that "[a]bove all it is this relationship between animal magnetism and death which deserves the very best attention" (357, my translation). This relationship is precisely what Schelling is exploring here. Although Franz Anton Mesmer (1733-1815) discovered animal magnetism, Mesmer's own interest lay in magnetism's alleged therapeutic value and the physical, rather than psychological, basis for its supposed success. He did not believe in any occult or paranormal interpretation of his work. Rather, he thought that just as the waves were pulled by the moon, so, too, were the fluids in the human body. The Romantics reinterpreted mesmerism so that the magnetized person's consciousness was understood to be enhanced and to be able to gain access to new worlds (Gerabek 1995, 98-99). Marquis de Puységur (1715-1825), Mesmer's pupil, later placed emphasis on the state of consciousness attained in the magnetic state and thus discovered somnambulism (Puységur 1811). Puységur appreciated that it was important for the magnetizer to be confident about the method, but he did not make the further connection that perhaps the patient was the one who needed to be confident. Unlike the Romantics, though, Puységur denied any occult interpretations of the state. When he used the word *clairvoyance*, it was in its literal sense of "clarity of sight" rather than an admittance of any paranormal origin (Beloff 1993). In 1814 Abbé Faria (or Joseph Custodius) postulated that Mesmer's phenomena were due to suggestion and he accepted the possibility of paranormal phenomena. James Braid, the father of hypnotism, then later placed the emphasis on the autosuggestibility of the patient (Schott 1985). Thus, Schelling's treatment of magnetism here is heavily influenced by the early Romantic tradition.

7. Mesmer supported his magnetizing sessions with music because he believed that music could carry magnetism. Mesmer's favored instrument was a harmonica (Gerabek 1995, 96). Thus the reference here to a harmonica itself suggests a transitional state. Throughout this passage Schelling is deliberately merging death with magnetic sleep.

8. The statue of Jupiter at Olympia was one of the seven wonders of the world. Jupiter, the sky god, was identified with the Greek Zeus. The Greeks believed that the body had value as well as the mind and thus both should be disciplined. Only thus could one truly honor Zeus. The statue at Olympia reputedly had carvings of other gods, mythical figures, sphinxes, and winged figures of victory round about Zeus's feet.

9. As Kuhlenbeck (1913) remarks, Schelling had continually protested against this understanding of his doctrine of identity.

10. This is the famous myth of Er in Plato's *Republic*, book 10. When left on the funeral pyre, Er reports what he experienced when he almost died. He tells of souls going to one of two places—either one of punishment or one of reward. Afterwards, perhaps after centuries, they return to a meadow. Souls can then choose their next life. Er

remarks that those who have been to the heavenly place and have had no suffering are usually not wise enough to choose a life of virtue, whereas those who descended to the place of punishment return to choose more wisely. Thus souls continually learn from one life to the next.

11. Schelling is referring to Swedenborg. For a discussion of Swedenborg's relevance to Schelling's work, with particular emphasis on *Clara*, see, e.g., Horn (1997).

12. Although now largely unknown, the haunting of the actress Hypollite Clairon referred to here was a hot topic of debate for almost thirty years. The account was first published in 1794 in Henri Meister's *Correspondance Littéraire* and again in 1798, both in Mlle Clairon's own memoires and in German translation. The case was as follows: At the height of Mlle Clairon's fame, a certain Mr. S, who was spending his money in the hope of coming into higher social circles, entered into her circle of acquaintances. Mlle Clairon regarded him only as a friend, whereas he read more into the relationship. On realizing that Mr. S wanted more than just friendship, Mlle Clairon arranged that he should see less of her to try and let him down gently. Disappointed, Mr. S became ill. Mlle Clairon helped out with his medical costs but still refused to see him, as she regarded this the best course of action. Two and a half years after their first meeting, Mr. S asked Mlle Clairon to visit him once more, on his deathbed. She refused. That very same evening at 11:00 P.M., which was the time that Mlle Clairon's acquaintances usually gathered at her place, a terrifying scream went through the room and was heard by all those present. This scream subsequently repeated itself on numerous occasions, always at the same time of night and always when Mlle. Clairon was present. Even the police were witness to this event. After some months the sound of the scream was replaced by the sound of gunfire, although no bullets could ever be found. She once felt a clip round her ear that accompanied the sound of the shot, and it always occurred at about 11:00 P.M. The gunfire then itself eventually became replaced by the sound of hands applauding and then fading into melodic sounds. After two and a half years—the same length of time as the duration of her friendship with Mr. S—the strange occurrences ceased. Some time afterward she happened to meet the servant who had been with Mr. S when he died. The servant related that when Mlle Clairon had refused to see Mr. S on his deathbed, Mr. S had exclaimed, "[S]he won't gain anything by that, I will pursue her after my death for as long as I have pursued her in life!" He had died shortly after 10.30 P.M. This whole set of events caused much controversy at the time.

This story was reproduced in many literary forms, including a relatively close adaptation of it in Goethe's "Geschichte von der Sängerin Antonelli" ("Story of the Singer Antonelli") in his *Unterhaltungen deutscher Ausgewanderten* (*Conversations among German Exiles*). For more information about Mlle Clairon's story and its literary reception, see Schmidt–von Essen (1994).

13. Here again Schelling may be thinking of Heinrich Stilling. In 1808 Jung-Stilling published *Theorie der Geister-Kunde*. The book caused a big stir at the time and was banned in some areas. Other countries approved of it and promoted it (Hahn 1990). Among other things, Jung-Stilling mentions cases where people who are sick and who long to see a particular person, fall into a trance and then appear to the person at the distant location (Jung-Stilling 1979, § 100; Shepard 1978). In § 204 Jung-Stilling hypothesizes that a being from the spirit world can come to know about someone's approaching death, for "the departed soul is where it loves."

14. Benz (1955) notes that Schelling often uses the expression "the ancients say" [*die Alten sagen*] to refer to Oetinger.

15. Homer's *Odyssey*, book 11.

IV

1. This passage is generally understood to be a critique of Hegel's *Phenomenology of Spirit*.

2. Saul had a religious conversion on the way to Damascus (Acts 9). After his conversion he devoted himself to preaching; he was a very successful speaker, able to appeal to many different types of people. Presumably, this is what Schelling wanted to promote—a voice for the public rather than a voice just for the philosophers.

3. This is where Ehrenberg's (1922) version of *Clara* ends.

V

1. The term *wirklich* is also connected to the verb *wirken*—to have an effect. *Abgeschlossenheit* also means something that is finished, completed. Thus, here Schelling is contrasting these two words.

2. This may be a reference to the third part of Kant's (1755) "Allgemeine Naturgeschichte und Theorie des Himmels" ["General Natural History and Theory of the Heavens"]. This third part discusses inhabitants of other stars. Kant speculates that at death the soul may live on other, distant planets, and he writes, "Does the immortal soul have to remain attached to this point in space all the time, for the entire endlessness of its future duration. . . . Should it never enjoy a closer look at the other wonders of creation. Who knows whether it isn't destined to get to know those spheres in the world's edifice" (my translation). However, Kant also says one could justifiably mock such ideas and that nobody would ground their hope for their future life on such flights of fancy.

Alternatively, Gauld (1992, 150) writes that somnambulists often gave accounts of trips to distant planets, and even more of them would claim to take trips to heaven or to see the spirits of the dead. These two facets of magnetic sleep merged into the idea that after death one's spirit went to a distant planet; but, Gauld says, although this view was probably around by 1811, it did not tend to find itself in print. Thus, Schelling, with his clear interest in magnetic sleep in *Clara*, may well have been commenting on these nondocumented views of the time.

3. See Acts 2 and 1 Corinthians, 14.2.

4. St. Walderich was a Benedictine monk and founded a cloister in Murrhardt, Baden-Wuertemmberg, in 817. Between 1220 and 1230 a chapel was erected in his memory. This is the chapel to which Schelling was referring in this episode. This chapel serves even now as a place of pilgrimage for many Catholics.

5. Two examples of oracles tied to a place are the Oracle of Delphos and the Oracle of Delos. The Oracle of Delphos came about because a goatherd saw his goats leaping about

strangely and making odd noises as they were feeding on Mt. Parnassus. The goatherd went up to them and then himself started to make peculiar movements and to make prophesies. Others, too, experienced this when they went to this area and so the Oracle of Delphos was set up. The Oracle of Delos, so the story goes, was set up on the authority of two doves, one of which had flown to the Temple of Jupiter Ammon and the other to Dodon. The doves spoke with a human voice to announce that Jupiter had chosen the area as a place for giving oracles.

SPRING

1. The spring fragment isn't present at all in the Kuhlenbeck (1913), Ehrenberg (1922), or Dietzfelbinger (1997) versions of *Clara*.

2. In K. F. A. Schelling: *Unserm Herzen genügt das bloße Geisterleben nicht* [The mere experience of spirit/mere ghostly life does not satisfy our heart]; in Schröter: *Unserm Herzen genügt das bloße Geistesleben nicht* [The mere mental and spiritual life does not satisfy our heart].

Glossary

GERMAN/ENGLISH

aufheben mit	to do away with
allerdings	certainly
das Äußerliche	external (appearance)
äußere	external
auflösen	to unravel, fuse, disintegrate
die Abgeschiedenen	our departed ones
die Aufhebung	raise up
aufheben	to annul
sich bemächtigen	to take hold
das Band	tie
das Band auflösen	to break the tie
der Begriff	idea
Bezug	reference
Bestimmtheit	certitude
sich durchdringen	to suffuse with
von etwas durchdrungen sein	to be suffused by
Dasein	existence
dunkel	dark; dark and obscure
das dunkle Gefühl	the vague feeling
das Entgegengesetzte	its opposite
etwas entgegengesetzt sein	to be opposed to something
erheben	to raise
sich erheben	to rise (up)
die Erhebung	elevation
die Erkenntnis	knowledge
erkennen	recognize, cognize
die Empfindung	feeling, sensibility
eigentlich	actually

eigentliches Selbst	*real self*
in etwas eingreifen	*to reach into*
einwickeln	*to entangle*
die entflohene Seele	*departed soul*
Das Entschlafen	*last sleep*
Entschlafene (die Entschlafenen)	*those who have been put to sleep; those having their last sleep*
Eingeschlafene	*those who have fallen asleep*
das Erwachen	*awakening*
die Erscheinung	*sign (of life);*
dunkle Erscheinung	*mysterious phenomenon*
die Erscheinungen	*phenomenon*
die Erkenntnis	*knowledge*
das Erkannte	*what is cognized*
der feinere Leib	*more subtle body*
festhalten	*to retain*
finster	*grim*
das fortdauernde Leben	*continuation of life*
Fortdauer	*survival*
freilich	*of course*
Gegenstände	*matters*
sich in etwas geben	*to merge into*
das Gefühl	*feeling*
die Geistreichen	*those who are spiritually and mentally rich*
in der gegenwärtigen Natur	*here within nature*
Geisterwelt	*spirit world*
das Geistige	*the spiritual*
geistige Welt	*spiritual world*
das Gemüt	*mind*
die Grenze	*division*
die Gestalt	*form*
die Gewalt	*force*
Grund(-lage)	*basis*
heiter	*bright, bright and cheerful*
hervorbringen	*bring forth*
heilig	*sacred*
das Höhere	*the higher*
höhere Bezeichnung	*higher description*
das höhere Geistige	*what is more highly spiritual*
das höhere Ganze	*greater whole*
höhere Gewissheit	*greater certainty*

GLOSSARY

hervordringen	to push through
hervortreten	to emerge
hervorbringend	creative
hervorbrechen	to burst forth
innig	profound
unser Inneres	our inner being
das Innere	internal/internality
innen	inner
innerlich	internal, inward
ein Inneres	internality
das Innerlichste	innermost
das Innerste	innermost being
die jenseitige Welt	the world beyond
im jetzigen Leben	in our present life
das jetzige Leben	our current life
Keim	germ
knüpfen	to bind
Kraft, Macht	power (strength mit Körper)
Kreis der Himmlischen	celestial sphere
Wechselspiel der Kräfte	interplay of forces
lebhaft	intense
Lebenskreis	
Licht werden	to become clear and light
Macht	power
mächtig	compelling; powerful
massiv	solid
Materie	matter
mitnichten	in no way, by no means
niederhalten	hold down
die Naturkräfte	natural forces
das Niedere	the lower
das Reden, die Rede	speech
in sich schließen	to embrace
die Schwärmerei	fanciful imagination
dies nie seiende Sein	this being that never actively is
das Seiende	what actively is

das Sein	beingness
Sein (no article)	being
Nichtsein (no article)	not being
selig	blessed
Seligkeit	bliss
Sinnenwelt	sensible world
sich steigern zu	to turn into
still	quiet
die Stille	peace
der Stoff	material, substance
der Träger	vessel
das Tier	animal life
der Umlauf	rotation
der Untergang	decline
übergehen in	to pass over to
der Übergang	transition
die Übermacht	superior strength
die Unauflöslichkeit	indissolubility
das Untergeordnete	the subordinate
unmittelbar	directly; immediately
sich vergeistigen	to become more spiritual
die Verbindung	link
die Verkettung	interconnection
vereinigen	to unite
das Verhältnis	relationship
verzaubert	bewitched
verzückt	enraptured
die Verstorbenen	the deceased
die Versetzung	transfer
verschlingen	to devour
sich verbinden	to bond
sich versichern	to procure
vorzüglicher Verstand	excellent mind
die Vorstellung	idea
wahr	truly
Wesen	essence, being or essence
unser Wesen	our essence
das Wesen	being
die Wesen (pl)	beings
dem Wesen nach	in its essence

in allen Wesen	*in all beings*
wir Wesen	*we beings*
die Willkür	*autocracy, spontaneity*
wild	*wild, unruly*
das Wirkliche	*what is real*
der Widerspruch	*contradiction*
wunderbar	*wonderful, astonishing*
sich zeigen	*to emerge*
zerfallen	*disintegrate*
zufällig	*chance*
ein zukünftiges Leben	*a life hereafter*
Zusammenhang	*connection, framework*
zurücksinken	*sinking back*
beschaulicher Zustand	*contemplative state*

ENGLISH/GERMAN

a life hereafter	*ein zukünftiges Leben*
actually	*eigentlich*
animal life	*das Tier*
annul	*aufheben*
astonishing	*wunderbar*
autocracy	*die Willkür*
awakening	*das Erwachen*
basis	*Grundlage*
being	*das Wesen; Sein (no article)*
beingness	*das Sein*
beings	*die Wesen (pl)*
in all beings	*in allen Wesen*
innermost being	*das Innerste*
our inner being	*unser Inneres*
bewitched	*verzaubert*
to bind	*knüpfen*
blessed	*selig*
bliss	*Seligkeit*
body (more subtle)	*der Leib (feiner)*
to bond	*sich verbinden*
bright	*heiter*
to bring forth	*hervorbringen*

to burst forth	hervorbrechen
by no means	mitnichten
certainly	allerdings
certitude	Bestimmtheit
chance	zufällig
cheerful	heiter
to become clear and light	Licht werden
to cognize	erkennen
compelling	mächtig
connection	Zusammenhang
contemplative state	beschaulicher Zustand
continuation of life	das fortdauernde Leben
contradiction	der Widerspruch
creative	hervorbringend
our current life	das jetzige Leben
the deceased	die Verstorbenen
decline	der Untergang
departed soul	die entflohene Seele
to disintegrate	zerfallen, auflösen
to devour	verschlingen
directly	unmittelbar
to do away with	aufheben mit
to embrace	in sich schließen
to emerge	sich zeigen, hervortreten
enraptured	verzückt
to entangle	einwickeln
essence	Wesen
in its essence	dem Wesen nach
excellent mind	vorzüglicher Verstand
existence	Dasein
external (appearance)	das Äußerliche, das Äußere
fanciful imagination	die Schwärmerei; dies nie seiende Sein
feeling	das Gefühl, die Empfindung
force	die Gewalt
interplay of forces	Wechselspiel der Kräfte
(in relation to nature)	(hervorbringende Kraft der Natur)
form	die Gestalt
framework	Zusammenhang
to fuse	auflösen

germ	Keim
greater certainty	höhere Gewissheit
greater whole	das höhere Ganze
grim	finster
here within nature	in der gegenwärtigen Natur
the higher	das Höhere
higher description	höhere Bezeichnung
to hold down	niederhalten
idea	die Vorstellung, die Begriffe
immediately	unmittelbar
in no way	mitnichten
indissolubility	die Unauflöslichkeit
inner	inner
our inner being	unser Inneres
innermost	das Innerlichste
innermost being	das Innerste
intense	lebhaft
interconnection	die Verkettung
internal/internality	das Innere
internal, inward	innerlich
knowledge	die Erkenntnis
last sleep	entschlafen
our current life	das jetzige Leben
(in our present) life	(im) jetzigen Leben
sphere of life	Lebenskreis
link	die Verbindung
the lower	das Niedere
matter	Materie
matters	Gegenstände
to merge into	sich in etwas geben
mind	das Gemüt
mysterious phenomenon	dunkle Erscheinung
natural forces	die Naturkräfte
not being	Nichtsein (no article)
to be opposed to something	etwas entgegengesetzt sein
its opposite	das Entgegengesetzte
our departed ones	die Abgeschiedenen

our essence	unser Wesen
of course	freilich, selbstverständlich
to pass over to	übergehen in
peace	die Stille
phenomenon	die Erscheinung
power	Macht
power (strength mit *Körper*)	Kraft, Macht
powerful	mächtig
to procure	sich versichern
profound	innig
to push through	hervordringen
quiet	still
to raise	erheben
raise up	die Aufhebung
raised	erhoben
to reach into	in etwas eingreifen
to recognize	erkennen
reference	Bezug
relationship	das Verhältnis
to retain	festhalten
to rise (up)	sich erheben
rotation	der Umlauf
sacred	heilig
seed	Keim
sensibility	die Empfindung
sensible world	Sinnenwelt
sign	die Erscheinung
sinking back	zurücksinken
solid	massiv
speech	das Reden, die Rede
sphere of life	Lebenskreis
spirit world	Geisterwelt
to become more spiritual	sich vergeistigen
spiritual world	geistige Welt
the spiritual	das Geistige
spontaneity	die Willkür
the subordinate	das Untergeordnete
substance	der Stoff
substantive being	das Sein
to suffuse with	durchdringen

to be suffused by	*von etwas durchdrungen sein*
superior strength	*die Übermacht*
survival	*Fortdauer*
to take over	*sich bemächtigen*
those who are spiritually rich	*die Geistreichen*
those who have been put to sleep; those having their last sleep	*Entschlafene (die Entschlafenen)*
those who have fallen asleep	*Eingeschlafene*
tie	*das Band*
to break the tie	*das Band (auf)lösen*
transfer	*die Versetzung*
transition	*der Übergang*
truly	*wahr*
to turn into	*sich steigern zu*
to unite	*vereinigen*
to unravel	*auflösen*
unruly	*wild*
the vague feeling	*das dunkle Gefühl*
vessel	*der Träger*
we beings	*wir Wesen*
what actively is	*das Seiende*
what is cognized	*das Erkannte*
what is more highly spiritual	*das höhere Geistige*
what is real	*das Wirkliche*
wonderful	*wunderbar*
the world beyond	*die jenseitige Welt*
wild	*wild*

REFERENCES

Beck, Otto. "Marginalien zur Geschichte des Kartäuserordens." *Der heilige Bruno.* Ed. Gerado Posada. Cologne: Wienand, 1987.

Beckers, Hubert. *Die Unsterblichkeitslehre Schellings im ganzen Zusammenhang ihrer Entwicklung.* Munich: Verlag der k. Akademie, 1865.

Beloff, John. *Parapsychology: A Concise History.* London: Athlone, 1993.

Benz, Ernst. *Schellings theologische Geistesahnen.* Wiesbaden: Verlag der Akademie der Wissenschaft und der Literatur in Mainz in Kommission bei Franz Steiner Verlag, 1955.

Borlinghaus, Ralph. *Neue Wissenschaft: Schelling und das Projekt einer positiven Philosophie.* Frankfurt am Main: Lang, 1994.

Braun, Otto. *Schelling als Persönlichkeit: Briefe, Reden, Aufsätze.* Leipzig: Eckardt, 1908.

Brown, Robert F. "Is much of Schelling's *Freiheitsschrift* (1809) already present in his *Philosophie und Religion?*" *Schellings Weg zur Freiheitsschrift: Legende und Wirklichkeit.* Eds. Hans Michael Baumgartner and Wilhelm G. Jacobs. Stuttgart-Bad Cannstatt: Frommann-Holzboog, 1996.

Dietzfelbinger, Konrad, ed. *Clara: Über den Zusammenhang der Natur mit der Geisterwelt.* By F. W. J. Schelling. Andechs, Germany: Dingfelder, 1987.

Ehrenberg, Hans, ed. "On Immortality" ("Über Unsterblichkeit"). By Ehrenberg. *Clara: Oder über den Zusammenhang der Natur mit der Geisterwelt.* By F. W. J. Schelling. Stuttgart: Frommanns, 1922.

Ehrhardt, Walter E. "Nachwort des Herausgebers." *Urfassung der Philosophie der Offenbarung.* Ed. Walter Ehrhardt. Hamburg: Meiner, 1992.

Ehrhardt, Walter E. "Goethes Clausthaler Tochter?—Auguste Böhmer starb vor 200 Jahren." *Unser Harz* 48 (2000): 183-90.

Ehrhardt, Walter E. *Schellings Lehre über Fortdauer und künftiges Leben. Einige Bermerkungen zum Schluß der Vorlesung "Einleitung in die Philosophie."*

Fuhrmans, Horst, ed. *F. W. J. Schelling: Briefe und Dokumente.* 3 vols. Bonn: Grundmann, 1962, 1973, 1975.

Gauld, Alan. *A History of Hypnotism.* Cambridge: Cambridge UP, 1992.

Gerabek, Werner E. *Friedrich Wilhelm Joseph Schelling und die Medizin der Romantik.* Frankfurt: Lang, 1995.

Grau, Alexander. "*Clara:* Über Schellings gleichnamiges Fragment." *Zeitschrift für philosophische Forschung* 51 (1997): 590-610.

Gulyga, Arsenij. *Schelling: Leben und Werk.* Trans. Elke Kirsten. Stuttgart: Deutsche Verlags-Anstalt, 1989.

Hahn, Elke, ed. *Schellings Pyrmonter Elegie: Der Briefwechsel mit Eliza Tapp, 1849-1854.* Intro. Xavier Tilliette. Frankfurt am Main.: Klostermann, 2000.

Hahn, Otto W. *Johann Heinrich Jung-Stilling.* Zurich: Brockhaus, 1990.

Hegel, George Wilhelm Friedrich. Phänomenologie des Geistes. 1807. *Hegels Werke: Jubiläums Ausgabe.* Ed. G. Lasson. Band 2. Leipzig: Meiner, 1911.

Horn, Friedemann. "F. W. J. Schellings Lehre von den letzten Dingen." *Zeitschrift für Religions und Geistesgeschichte* 6 (1954): 254.

Horn, Friedemann. *Schelling and Swedenborg: Mysticism and German Idealism.* Trans. George F. Dole. West Chester, Pennsylvania: Swedenborg Foundation, 1997.

Jenny, E., A. Öhler, and H. Stauffer. *Basel Schweizerische Medizinische Wochenschrift* 66. (1936).

Jung-Stilling, Johann Heinrich. *Theorie der Geisterkunde.* 1808. Afterword by M. Titzmann. Hildesheim: Gerstenberg, 1979.

Kahn-Wallerstein, Carmen. *Schellings Frauen: Caroline und Pauline.* Bern: Francke, 1959.

Kant, Immanuel. (1755). "Allgemeine Naturgeschichte und Theorie des Himmels." *Kants Werke.* Ed. Königlich Preußischen Akademie der Wissenschaften. Band I. Berlin: Reimer, 1910. 215-368.

Kirchhoff, Jochen. *Schelling.* Reinbek bei Hamburg: Rowohlt Taschenbuch, 1982.

Kleßmann, Eckart. *Caroline.* Munich: List, 1975.

Knatz, Lothar, Hans Jörg Sandkühler, and Martin Shraven, eds. *F. W. J. Schelling: Philosophische Entwürfe und Tagebücher 1809-1813.* Hamburg: Meiner, 1994.

Kovács, Elisabeth. "Joseph II und die Aufhebung der kontemplativen Klöster in der österreichischen Monarchie." *Symposium über die Kartäusergeschichte und spiritualität.* Ed. James Hogg. Salzburg: Institut für Anglistik und Amerikanistik, 1984.

Kuhlenbeck, Ludwig, ed. Foreword. *Clara: oder über den Zusammenhang der Natur mit der Geisterwelt.* By F. W. J. Schelling. Leipzig: Reclam, 1913.

Lavater, Johann Kaspar. *Aussichten in die Ewigkeit: In Briefen an Herrn Joh. George Zimmermann.* 4 vols. Zurich: Drell, 1778.

Melton, John Gordon, ed. *Encyclopedia of Occultism and Parapsychology.* 2 vols. Detroit: Gale Research, 1996.

Pareyson, Luigi, ed. *Schellingiana Raroria.* Torino: Bottega d'Erasmo, 1977.

Pfau, Thomas, ed. and trans. *Idealism and the Endgame of Theory.* Albany: State U of New York P, 1996.

Plitt, Gustav L., ed. *Aus Schellings Leben: In Briefen.* 3 vols. Leipzig: Verlag von S. Hirzel, 1869.

Puységur, Armand Marie Jacques. *Recherches, expériences et observations physiologiques sur l'homme dans l'état de somnambulisme naturel et dans le somnambulisme provoqué par l'acte magnétique.* Paris: Dentu, 1811.

Ritchie, Gisela F. *Caroline Schlegel-Schelling in Wahrheit und Dichtung.* Bonn: Bouvier, 1968.

Sandkühler, Hans Jörg, ed. *F. W. J. Schelling.* Stuttgart: Metzler, 1998.

Schelling, Karl Friedrich August, ed. *F. W. J. von Schellings sämmtliche Werke*. 10 + 4 vols. *On Nature's Connection to the Spirit World* is in vol. 9. Stuttgart: Cotta, 1856-1861. 1-110.

Schelling, Friedrich Wilhelm Joseph. *Of Human Freedom*. 1809. Trans. James Gutmann. Illinois: Open Court, 1936.

Schelling, Friedrich Wilhelm Joseph. *The Ages of the World*. 1815 draft. Trans. Frederick de Wolfe Bolman, Jr. New York: Columbia UP, 1942.

Schelling, Friedrich Wilhelm Joseph. *Bruno: or, on the Natural and the Divine Principle of Things*. 1802. Trans. Michael Vater. Albany: State U of New York P, 1984.

Schelling, Friedrich Wilhelm Joseph. *Of Human Freedom*. 1809. Trans. Patricia Hayden-Roy. *Philosophy of German Idealism*. Ed. Ernst Behler. New York: Continuum, 1987.

Schelling, Friedrich Wilhelm Joseph. *Ages of the World*. 1813 draft. Trans. Judith Norman. *The Abyss of Freedom: Ages of the World*. Ed. Slavoj Zizek. Ann Arbor: U Michigan P, 1997.

Schelling, Friedrich Wilhelm Joseph. *The Ages of the World*. 1815 draft. Trans. Jason M. Wirth. Albany: State U of New York P, 2001.

Schmidt-von Essen, Maren I. *Mademoiselle Clairon: Verwandlungen einer Schauspielerin*. Frankfurt: Lang, 1994.

Schönwitz, Ute. "Schellings Paten." *Friedrich Wilhelm Schelling Raum*. Stadt Leonberg, Schul-, Kultur- und Sportamt, 1992. Booklet from the Schelling museum, Leonberg, Germany.

Schott, Heinz. "Mesmers Heilungskonzept und seine Nachwirkungen in der Medizin." *Franz Anton Mesmer und die Geschichte des Mesmerismus*. Ed. Heinz Schott. Stuttgart: Steiner, 1985/

Schubert, Gotthilf Heinrich. *Ansichten von der Nachtseite der Wissenschaft*. Dresden: Arnoldische Buchhandlung, 1808.

Shepard, Leslie A. *Encyclopedia of Occultism and Parapsychology*. 2 vols. Detroit: Gale Research, 1978.

Tilliette, Xavier. *Schelling: Une Philosophie en Devenir*. 2 vols. Paris: Libraire philosophique J. Vrin, 1970.

Tilliette, Xavier, ed. *Schelling im Spiegel seiner Zeitgenossen*. 2 vols. Torino: Bottega d'Erasmo, 1974, 1981.

Tilliette, Xavier. *Schelling: biographie*. Paris: Calmann-Lévy, 1999.

Vetö, Miklos, ed. *Stuttgarter Privatvorlesungen: version inéd., accompagnée du texte des oeuvres*. Turin: Bottega d'Erasmo, 1973.

Waitz, Georg, ed. *Caroline: Briefe aus der Frühromantik*. 2 vols. Expanded by Erich Schmidt. Leipzig: Insel, 1913.

Walter, François. *Bedrohliche und bedrohte Natur: Umweltgeschichte der Schweiz seit 1800*. Trans. Béatrice Raboud, Peter Kamber, and Katharina Belser. Zurich: Chronos, 1996.

White, Alan. *Schelling: An Introduction to the System of Freedom*. New Haven: Yale UP, 1983.

Index

accidental, 27, 28. *See also* chance
Achilles, 60
Agricole, 91
Albert (Clara's loved one), xi, xxix, xxxiii, xxxiv, 11, 21, 64
Allgemeine Literaturzeitung, xxv
Anderson, Penny, xl
animal magnetism, xiv, xxvi, 93. *See also* magnetic sleep
appearance, 22, 25, 27-8, 40, 67, 72, 77
    external appearance, 10, 17-18, 37, 48
art, 7, 16-17, 28, 65-6, 70, 77
    artist, 17, 54, 68, 70, 80
    artistic, 16
Auguste (Caroline's daughter). *See* Böhmer, Auguste

basis, 5-6, 23, 27-8, 49, 54, 65, 73. *See also* root
Baur, Daniele, xxxix
Beck, Otto, 91
Beckers, Hubert, xiii, xv-xvi
beginning, 3-7, 15, 22, 36, 39, 50, 61, 79
beingness, 19, 42-3, 52, 54, 58
belief, 4, 6, 10, 19, 56, 60, 70, 74, 78
Beloff, John, 93
Benz, Ernst, 92, 95
bewitched, 38, 58
    bewitching, 57. *See also* magic; spell
birth, 61, 80
blessed, 16, 43, 47, 51-2, 58, 60, 67, 75, 80
bliss, 16, 31-2, 44, 54-5, 79, 83
body, 12, 16, 19, 24, 33-42, 44, 48-50, 54, 56-9, 72, 77, 80, 90, 92
    foreign body, xxxvi

subtle body, 40, 92
    See also corporeality
Böhm, Gabriela, xxxix
Böhme, Jakob, xxvi
Böhmer, Auguste, xiv, xix-xxix, xxxiii-xxxiv, 89-90
Böhmer, Georg, xx
Böhmer, Johann, xix
Böhmer, Therese, xix
Bonaventura, xiii, xxv, 89
Borlinghaus, Ralph, xii
Braid, James, 93
Braun, Otto, xxxvi
Brown, John, xxii-xxiii
Brown, Robert F, xxxv

Campetti, xxvi, 92
Catholic, ix, 11, 74, 90, 95
center, 31-2, 69
certainty, 5-6, 13, 31, 33, 68
chain, 4, 32, 53. *See also* link
chance, 14, 24, 27, 37, 40, 50, 55. *See also* accidental
charm, 25, 44, 65. *See also* magic; spell
Christ, 61
Clairon, Hypollite, 56, 94
clairvoyance, ix, xi, xiv, xxvi, xxxiv-xxxv, 48-9, 51, 55, 57-8, 72, 83, 92
Clara of Assisi, xxxiv
Clärchen, xxxiv-xxxv
Condillac, Etienne Bonnot de, 92
connection, 3-6, 12-3, 25, 27, 35, 49, 58. *See also* link; tie
consciousness, 36, 48, 49-51, 55
constancy, 16, 32
constant, 24, 32, 75

111

contradiction, 7, 14, 27, 45. *See also* opposite
corporeality, 38, 41, 49-50, 54, 56, 73, 77, 80
  corporeal, 38-41, 55-8, 68, 71, 76-8, 80 *See also* body
Cotta, Johann Friedrich, xiv, xvii, xxvi
creation, 23, 76
crisis, 21, 24

dead, 10, 12, 47, 49, 52, 57, 63, 71-2
  the dead, 9, 60-1, 73, 90, 95. *See also* departed
death, 9, 12, 14-15, 24, 64, 71, 76, 79, 90, 92-5
  force/power of, 22-3, 61
  life after, 18, 33, 54-9, 67-8
  moment of, 46-49
  preparation towards, 16, 44
  transition from life to, 36-42, 45, 49-52
deceased, 10, 12, 46, 73
departed, 31, 46. *See also* dead
desire, 3, 21, 51, 54, 59, 72, 75, 77, 80
destiny, 13, 32, 77. *See also* fate
destructive, 23-5, 50, 72
development, 24, 27, 31-2, 40, 59, 61, 71
Dietzfelbinger, Konrad, 96
divine, 14, 27-8, 31, 33, 44, 48, 54, 58, 64, 70, 76, 78, 81, 90
  denial of, 4, 6
  hand of, 24, 60
  the divine, 46, 51-3
dream, 18, 47, 55, 58, 92
Duggar, Delpha, xl
duty, 10, 12-13, 27

Earth, 25, 31-2, 46, 60-61, 68-9, 71, 76-8, 90
Ecce Homo, 63
Ehrenberg, Hans, xxxviii, 95-96
Ehrhardt, Walter, E., xv, xxxiii, xxxv, xl, 89-91
element, 32, 41, 71, 77
  elements, 76. *See also* potencies; powers
end, 5, 10, 17, 19, 22, 27, 37, 51, 55, 65, 70, 76, 78
Er, myth of, 93
Eschenmayer, Carl August, xxv

essence, 5, 7, 13-14, 22-3, 41, 60, 77-9, 81
  mediating essence, 33-4, 38, 40
  spiritual-corporeal essence, 57-8
  spiritual essence, 42, 49-50, 54, 72
eternity, 28, 63
  eternal, 9, 14-15, 19, 24, 51, 61, 63, 67, 70, 80
  eternally, 14, 18-19, 36, 55, 67
evil, 26, 55, 56, 57, 59
external, 5, 24-9, 40-6, 54-7, 65, 71-2, 76, 78-9, 81

Falkenhagen, Harriet, xxxix
Fall, the, 26-7
fanciful imagination, 5-6, 15
Faria, Abbé Joseph Custodius, 93
fate, 10, 18, 26, 40, 47, 75-6, 79-80. *See also* destiny
feeling, 6, 11, 14, 16, 26-7, 46, 57-9, 73, 83
  differing from knowledge, 7, 15, 31-2
  qua intuition, 4, 21, 69, 76
Fichte, Johann Gottlieb, xviii, 92
fire, 24, 26, 28, 52, 66, 81
force, 12, 14, 16, 22-3, 27, 40, 44, 57, 61, 72. *See also* power
foreign, 18, 23, 27, 44, 51
Forster, Georg, xix
Francis of Assisi, xxxiv
free, 14, 16-17, 23-4, 26-8, 40, 44, 49, 57, 59-60, 71, 80
freedom, 14-15, 17, 24, 28, 44, 57-8, 65, 73, 80
French Revolution, xviii, 91
Fuhrmans, Horst, xxxvii
future, 68, 95
  the future, 21, 26, 46, 49, 67

Gauld, Alan, 95
Georgii, Eberhard Friedrich, xxix-xxxi
Gerabek, Werner E., xxii, 93
germ, 36, 40, 42, 44, 46, 50-1, 53, 56, 59
Germany, 64, 91
  German, 17-18, 90, 94
God, 12, 14, 16, 19, 24, 27, 29, 32, 51-5, 59-60, 67, 69, 74-6, 78, 80
  as creator, 23, 61, 77

Goethe, Johann Wolfgang von, xix, xxii, xxiv, xxvii, xxxi, xxxiii–xxxiv, 89, 94
   Action at a Distance, xxxi
   Die Wahlverwandschaften [*The Elective Affinities*], xxvii
   Egmont, xxxiv
Gotter, Luise, xxvii–xxviii
Gotter, Pauline. *See* Schelling
Grau, Alexander, viii, xiv, xxxiv, xxxvi
Gulyga, Arsenij, xiii–xiv, xvi, xviii, xxi, xxxvi, 89

Haag, Ruth, 89
Hahn, Elke, xxxvii
Hahn, Otto W., 94
harmony, 3, 17, 40, 72, 92
heart, 13–18, 24, 27–9, 34, 47, 72, 74, 76, 78–80
heaven, 13–14, 26, 28–9, 65, 67–9, 75, 90, 93–4
   Earth and, 4–5, 24, 31, 61
   heavenly, 24, 29, 39, 40–1, 48, 71
   See also life; world
Hegel, Georg Wilhelm Friedrich, xiv, xviii, xxvi, xxxii, 92, 95
   Phenomenology of Spirit, xiv, xxvi
hell, 60
Heyne, Therese, xix
hidden, 13–14, 21–2, 25, 39–40, 46, 48, 59–60. *See also* secret; mystery
Hoffman, Ernst Theodor, xxxix
Hölderlin, Friedrich, xviii
Holmes, Veronica, xl
home, 12, 14, 19, 21, 26, 61, 72, 74
Homer, 60
Horn, Friedemann, x–xi, xiii, xxxiii, 90, 94
Hufeland, Christoph Wilhelm, xxii–xxiii

image, 31, 61, 69
immortality, 5, 13, 33, 36, 64. *See also* life; survival
individuality, 50–3. *See also* personality; self
influence, 7, 11, 47, 50, 56, 60, 72
inner being, 13–14, 19, 25–8, 47–8, 53, 55, 73, 75–7
innermost, 7, 28, 36, 42, 47, 76, 78
   innermost being, 4, 6–7, 21, 36, 60

internal, 29, 40, 42–7, 54, 57–8, 65, 71–2, 76, 78–9
internality, 43–5, 83
invisible, 14, 25, 55, 59, 67–8, 72

Joseph II, 91
Jung-Stilling, Johann Heinrich, 92, 94
Jupiter, 54, 93

Kahn-Wallenstein, Carmen, xiii, xxi–xxii, xxxvi
Kant, Immanuel, viii, 95
Kirchhoff, Jochen, xxxvi
Kleßmann, Eckart, xxi, xxxvi
Klingemann, Ernst August Friedrich, 89
Knatz, Lothar, 92
knowledge, 3–6, 15, 17, 21, 32, 43–4, 73, 81
Kovács, Elisabeth, 91
Kuhlenbeck, Ludwig, xiv, xxxvii, 90, 93

Lavater, Johann Kaspar, 92
law, 4, 13, 18, 24, 27, 60, 72, 78, 80
life
   higher life, 39, 46, 60
   next life, 15, 28, 42, 44, 46, 53–4, 73, 80, 93–5. *See also* death; immortality
   this life, 12, 32, 37–9, 42, 44–7, 54, 61, 73, 80
   See also spirit; spiritual; world
light, 4–5, 19, 25, 32, 47–8, 50–4, 59, 70, 75, 78, 80
limitations, 29, 32
link, 12–13, 19, 21, 24, 35–7, 50, 53, 75, 77. *See also* chain; connection
longing, 7, 13, 15, 18, 21, 27, 47, 79
love, 7, 12–14, 21, 27, 34, 39, 49, 52, 57, 59, 72

magic, 25, 28, 32, 74, 79. *See also* charm; spell
   magical, 12, 25, 34
magnetic sleep, 52–3, 93, 95
man, 4–6, 14–15, 32, 34, 38–9, 44, 47, 53, 60–1, 74, 76–7, 79
   his connection to nature, 19, 23–8, 75
Marcus, Adelbert Friedrich, xxxii

memory, 22, 33, 49, 71, 83. *See also* remember
Mesmer, Franz Anton, 93
Michaelis, Johann David, xix
Miener, Michael, xxxix
mind, 15, 18, 27, 56, 68
music, 48, 72, 78
mystery, 38. *See also* hidden; secret
  mysterious, 48
  mysteriousness, 67

nature, 3-5, 7, 13-19, 29, 33, 45, 47, 50, 53-4, 57
  as destructive, 21-7
  as external, 40-2, 58, 60, 70, 79-80
  as subordinated, 68, 41
necessity, 4, 14-15, 22, 27-8, 32, 43
  necessary, 3, 24, 33, 40-1, 44-5, 48, 52, 58, 63, 65-6, 70, 74, 77-8
Niethammer, Friedrich Immanuel, xix, xxv, 89
night, 13, 19, 46-7, 55, 61, 74-5
Novalis, xix

obscurity, 28, 50, 55, 63
  obscure, 36, 39, 42, 49-51, 53, 60, 63
Oetinger, Friedrich Christoph, 92, 95
Old Testament, 60
opposite, 5, 6, 13, 16, 28, 35, 38, 55, 59, 63, 69, 80. *See also* contradiction
  opposed, 4, 33, 58-9, 68, 81
  opposites, 33-5, 68
  opposition, 29, 71
oracles, 75, 95

Pappenheim, Jenny von, 89
Paracelsus, 91
Pareyson, Luigi, xxxvii, 89
Pascal, Blaise, 63
passion, xxi, 12, 16, 54, 67, 92
past, 49, 64-7, 83
Paulus, Heinrich, xvii-xviii, xxv, 89
peace, 10, 15, 17-18, 60, 67, 76-7, 80, 83
perfection, 42, 45, 51-2, 70, 80-1
personality, 37, 49-50, 59, 64. *See also* individuality; self
Pfau, Thomas, 89

philosopher(s), 36-7, 44, 47, 63-6, 76, 78, 95
philosophy, 3-4, 6, 63-4
physical, 4, 6, 17, 34, 49-50, 53, 68, 73, 80. *See also* corporeal
planets, 77-8, 95
Plato, 17, 55, 93
Plihal, Werner, xxxix
Plitt, Gustav L., xxxvii
potency, 43, 46, 79
  potencies, 80
power, 14, 19, 27, 32, 45, 54, 57, 60, 65, 71, 79-81. *See also* force
powers, 13, 21, 25, 71, 79, 81. *See also* elements; principles; potencies
premonition, xxxv, 39, 54, 58, 92
present, 5, 15, 24, 27, 32-5, 37, 40, 42, 44, 46, 55-7, 68, 72, 80
  present (=gift), 14, 31
  present (verb), 63
  the present (=now), 38, 49, 64, 65
presentiment. *See* premonition
principles, 28. *See also* elements; potencies; powers
proof, 5-6, 13, 16, 33, 37, 47
prophecy, prophetic. *See* premonition
Protestant, 74, 90, 91
prototype, 68
pure, 13, 16, 23, 41, 44, 59, 71
Puységur, Armand Marie Jaques, 93

reality, 22, 27-8, 51, 61, 65, 80
  real, 5-7, 15, 21, 28, 32, 54, 65, 67-8, 76
reason, 7, 13, 32, 37-8, 64, 70, 77
Reinhold, Karl Leonhard, xii
relationship, 6, 11, 14-15, 37, 46, 50, 52, 66, 70, 75, 78
remember, 11, 14, 34, 38-40, 47, 54-5, 57, 64, 77. *See also* memory
revelation, 6, 29, 64, 78
Ritchie, Gisela F., xx
Ritter, Johann Wilhelm, xxvi, 92
river, 10, 17, 67, 90
Romanticism, vii, xix-xx, xxii, 93
root, 14-15, 21, 50, 59, 72. *See also* basis
Röschlaub, A., xxii
rotation, 35, 37, 39, 76

sanctuary, 11, 18, 61
Sandkühler, Hans Jörg, xxxvii
Saul, 64, 95
Scheer, Christian, xxxix
Schelling, Caroline, (wife) xiii–xvi,
  xix–xxxvii, 89–91
Schelling, Caroline (daughter), xxxii
Schelling, Clara, xxxii
Schelling, Friedrich Wilhelm Joseph von,
  vii, x–xxxvii, 90–2, 95
  Ages of the World, x–xi, xiii, xv–xvi, xxxi,
    xxxv, 89
  Bruno, xii–xv, xxv, 89
  Clara, vii, x, xii–xvii, xxiv, xxvi,
    xxviii–xxx, xxxiii, xxxv–xxxvii, 92
  Der Traum des Kirsos, xii
  *Epikurische Glaubensbekenntnisse Heinz
    Widersportens*, xxv
  Erlangen Seminars, xiii
  *Gespräch zwischen dem Verfasser und
    einem Freund*, xii
  Ideas on a Philosophy of Nature, xviii
  Of Human Freedom, x, xii, xiv, xxxv, 89
  *On the Possibility of a Form of Philosophy
    in General*, xviii
  On the True Concept of Natural Philosophy, xxv
  On the World Soul, xix
  *Philosophical Letters on Dogmatism and
    Criticism*, xviii
  Philosophie der Offenbarung, xxxi, xxxv
  Philosophie und Religion, xii, xiv, xxv, xxxv
  Philosophy of Mythology, xxxi
  Presentation of my Philosophical System, xxv
  Stuttgart Seminars, xiii, xv, xxxi, xxxv, 89
  System of Philosophy, xiii
Schelling, Hermann, xxxii
Schelling, Joseph, xxxii
Schelling, Karl Eberhard, xxii, xxvi
Schelling, Karl Friedrich August, x–xiii, xv,
  xxxii–xxxiv, xxxvii, 79, 96
Schelling, Paul, xxxii
Schelling, Pauline, xxvii–xxxvi
Schillemeit, Jost, 89
Schlegel, August Wilhelm, xvii, xix–xxv
Schlegel, Caroline. *See* Schelling
Schlegel, Friedrich, xix–xxiii
Schleiermacher, Friedrich, xxiii
Schmidt-von Essen, Maren I., 94
Schönwitz, Ute, xvii
Schott, Heinz, 93
Schröter, Manfred, xi, xxxvii–xxxix, 79, 96
Schubert, Gotthilf Heinrich, xiv, xxvi, 90,
  93
Schütz, Christian Gottfried, xxv
science, 3–7, 17, 25, 32, 65–6, 68, 83
sciences, 3, 5, 10, 16–17, 83
scientific, 5, 7, 17, 63, 78
Scottish Highlands, 75
secret, 11, 17, 22, 28, 75–6. *See also* hidden; mystery
self, 36, 50–1, 54–5, 78. *See also* individuality; personality
separation, 13, 24, 33, 37, 42, 49, 61, 66, 71
separate, 5, 13, 22, 55, 70, 79
separated, 11, 13, 33, 36, 51–2, 59, 71,
  79
Shepard, Leslie A., 91, 94
signs, 22, 26, 29, 39–40, 47, 67, 73
sin, 58, 83
sleep, 39, 46–8, 57–8, 74
Socrates, 60, 64, 71
sorrow, 21–2, 26
soul, 5, 17, 21, 29, 31, 50, 72, 76, 79, 90, 92
  bridging body and spirit, 33–40, 56–7
  its condition of clairvoyance, 47, 49, 59
  its unity with God, 14, 52
souls, 14, 31, 56, 58, 69, 71–2, 93–4
spell, 25
spellbinding, 26. *See also* bewitched;
  charm; magic
Spinoza, Baruch, xxv
spirit, 13–15, 17, 41, 54, 59, 64, 66, 75,
  79, 90, 95, 96
  its relation to the body, 12, 33–9, 57, 80
spirit life, 32, 37, 47, 67
spirit world, 3–5, 23–4, 28, 36, 50, 61,
  68, 73, 83, 94
spirits, 11, 25, 36, 41, 67, 74–5, 77, 83,
  95
spiritual, 11, 24, 29, 32–4, 37, 40, 42, 45,
  47–9, 51, 53–5, 57–8, 70, 75, 78
spiritual life, 17, 39, 61, 80
spiritual world, 4–5, 13, 60, 68, 71
the spiritual, 3–6, 13, 28, 38–9, 41, 50,
  56, 61, 68, 71–3, 76, 81, 92

spirituality, 13, 50, 56, 77, 80
Spix, Johann Baptist, xxx, 90
strength, 5, 11, 15, 21-2, 24-6, 29, 34, 41, 47, 53, 69, 70, 77
  inner strength, 27
subordinate, 5, 29, 39-40, 44-6, 56, 65, 68, 70, 72, 80
suffused, 43, 52-4, 76, 79
survival, 35-7, 47, 49. *See also* immortality, life, spirit world
Swedenborg, Emanuel, 56, 77, 94

talisman, 26
Thiry Years' War, 11, 77, 90-1
Thorvaldsen, Bertel, 89
tie, 4, 13, 14, 24, 33, 36, 40, 61, 73. *See also* connection; link
Tieck, Ludwig, xix, xxii
Tilliette, Xavier, xiii-xv, xxvi, xxxvii, 89, 92
Tischbein, Karoline, 89
transfiguration, 7, 24, 48, 55, 73, 76, 81
  transfigured, 31, 48, 52-3, 60, 73, 76, 79
transformation, 41, 47, 50, 52-3
  transformed, 21, 25-6, 46, 50-3, 80
transition, 4, 13, 24, 37-9, 71
transmigration of souls, 10, 37
truth, 7, 10, 16, 44, 60, 64, 81, 92

unconsciously, 21
unity, 33, 35-6, 49, 52-3, 65-6, 71, 79
  united, 4, 11, 32-3, 75, 79

Veit, Dorothea, xix, xxi-xxii
vessel, 50, 52, 61
Vetö, Miklos, xiii, xvi-xvii, 90, 92

Waitz, Georg, xxxvii, 91
Walderich, St, 74, 95
Walter, François, 91
what actively is, 42-3, 51-2, 54, 58
White, Alan, xii
whole, 9, 11-12, 16, 18, 52, 55, 68, 74,
  the whole, 14, 27, 40, 42, 70
  whole being, 32, 48-9
  whole of nature, 19, 22, 24, 60, 80
  whole person, 33-5, 38, 90
will, 14, 26, 29, 32, 39, 52-3, 57, 75, 93
  evil will, 56, 59
  self-will, 52
Windischmann, Karl Joseph Hieronymus, xxvi
Wirth, Jason, xxxix-xl
word, 7, 13-14, 24, 33, 43, 53, 58, 72-3, 77-9
world
  inner world, 55
  next world, 3, 12-13, 24, 27-8, 39, 68, 71, 75-6
  this world, 12, 24, 27-8, 49, 68, 71-2, 76, 78
worth, 27, 42, 72, 77

Zeus, 93
Ziegesar, Silvie, xxxi